Espresso with
Esther

Advancing the Ministries of the Gospel
AMG *Publishers*

God's Word to you is our highest calling.

SANDRA GLAHN

Coffee Cup Bible Studies
Espresso with Esther

© 2006 by Sandra L. Glahn

Published by AMG Publishers. All Rights Reserved.

Published in association with the literary
agency of Alive Communications, Inc., 7860 Goddard Street, Suite 200,
Colorado Springs, Colorado, 80920

Third Printing, 2012

ISBN: 0-89957-220-0

Editing and Proofreading: Rick Steele and Jonathan Wright
Interior Design: PerfecType, Nashville, Tennessee
Cover Design: Brian Woodlief at ImageWright Marketing and Design,
Chattanooga, Tennessee

Printed in the United States of America
16 15 14 13 12 –CH– 7 6 5 4 3

Dedicated to all my favorite nieces:

**Alisha, Devin, Erin, Heather,
Julia, Jordy, and Katie**

May you continue to be like Esther, beautiful in every way!

ACKNOWLEDGMENTS

No one who writes, particularly one who writes a Bible study, can possibly thank all the people who have influenced his or her work. If I were to try to do so, my list would be longer than the study itself. My mentors believed I could teach before I did, each opening doors to a variety of opportunities for me, for which I'm grateful. And my Washington Bible College and Dallas Theological Seminary professors all pointed out numerous truths I could take from the biblical text.

Two essential elements in writing, however, are to be concise and to avoid boring the reader. So I will limit my thanks to the following:

- to Gary, my husband, for his tenacious, loyal love and for believing I should teach and write occupationally long before I had any vision to do so (and for designing and keeping up with the web site)

- to Dr. Bob Chisholm for making Hebrew narrative come alive with the help of a little stand-up comedy

- to the "test group" at Creekside, now Rowlett Bible Fellowship, for their terrific feedback and their involvement with this study, including the Texas version of the kids' Purim pageant

- to Chip MacGregor, my agent, for helping me hone the series concept and finding a home for it

- to Virginia Swint and Karen Swint for always being available with extra sets of proofers' eyes

- to Rhonda Oglesby and Erin Teske along with the Virginia "Esther group" for providing a means by which readers can give artistic expression to their contemplations at **soulpersuit.com**

- to those who are praying that lives will be changed through interaction with the biblical text. You know who you are.

- to Dan Penwell and Rick Steele of AMG for their enthusiasm for the project, their commitment to excellence, and their generous encouragement along the way.

- to the wonderful, gifted staff of Biblical Studies Press (bible.org), translators of the NET Bible translation printed as the primary Scripture text in this book. Without the help of this essential ministry, the entire concept of the Coffee Cup Bible Studies would not have been possible.

- to God, in whom **all things** are possible!

INTRODUCTION TO THE COFFEE CUP BIBLE STUDIES

"The precepts of the LORD are right, rejoicing the heart;
The commandment of the LORD is pure, enlightening the eyes." (Psa. 19:8, NASB)

Congratulations! You have chosen wisely. By choosing to study the Bible, you are electing to spend time learning that which will rejoice the heart and enlighten the eyes.

And while any study in the Bible is time well spent, the Coffee Cup Bible Studies have some unique elements that set them apart from others. So before we get started, let's talk about some of those elements which will, we hope, help you maximize your study time.

Life Rhythms. Most participants in any Bible study have little problem keeping up during the weekdays, when they have a routine. Yet on the weekends there's a general "falling off." Thus, the Coffee Cup Bible Studies contain Monday-through-Friday Bible study questions, but the Saturday and Sunday segments consist of short, more passive readings that draw application and insight from the texts you'll be considering. Know that the days listed here are mere suggestions. Feel free to change the structure of days and assignments to best fit your own needs.

Community. The studies in the Coffee Cup series are ideal for group interaction. If you don't have a local group with which to meet, find a few friends and start one. Or connect with others through the Esther section of the author's Web site (www.aspire2.com) and an associated site (www.soulpersuit.com), where you can find and participate—if you like—by engaging in artistic expressions as you interact with the text. (These vehicles give you opportunities to share with a wider community what you're learning.) While each study is designed for group use, private questions not intended for group discussion appear in italics.

Aesthetics. One feature of the aforementioned Web sites are links to art that depict what's being discussed. For example, "Esther Before Ahasuerus" by Artemisia Gentileschi (1623)—one of the few female Renaissance painters—hangs in the Metropolitan Museum of Art in New York, and is accessible via a link on the web. Also on the sites, you'll find links to notes for further study. There'll be lists of DVDs you can buy or rent, such as the Veggie Tales movie, *The Girl Who Became Queen,* as well as novels based on the Esther story. You'll even find a recipe for Hamantashen. If you don't know what that is, you'll find that out, too. If you would like to interact artistically with your contemplations, you'll be challenged to consider creating a playing-card sized piece of art. (Something that small is relatively easy to fill, even for non-artists.) Engage all five senses in your interaction with God's truth!

Convenience. Rather than turning in the Bible to find the references, you'll find the entire text for each day included in the Coffee Cup study book. While it's important to know our way around the Bible, the Coffee Cup Bible Studies are designed this way so you can take them with you and study the Bible on the subway, at a coffee shop, in a doctors' waiting room, or on your lunch break. The chosen translation is the NET Bible, which is accessible via the Internet from virtually anywhere in the world. You can find more about it, along with numerous textual notes, at **bible.org** which serves 3.5 million people worldwide.

The NET Bible is a modern translation from the ancient Greek, Hebrew, and Aramaic texts. Alumni and friends of Dallas Theological Seminary make up the core group of individuals behind the site, particularly the NET Bible translation project. The Bible, both in its online and print versions, includes 60,932 translators' notes and citations originating from more than 700 scholarly works.

Sensitivity to time-and-culture considerations. Many Bible studies skip what we call the "theological" step. That is, they go straight from observing and interpreting the words given to those in a different time and culture to applying in a modern-day setting. The result is sometimes misapplication (such as, "Paul told slaves to obey their *masters* so we need to obey our *employers*"). In the Coffee Cup series, our aim is to be particularly sensitive to the audience to whom the "mail" was addressed and work to take the crucial step of separating what was intended for a limited audience from that which is for all audiences for all time (love God; love your neighbor).

Sensitivity to genres. Rather than crafting a series in which each study is structured exactly like all the others, each of the Coffee Cup Bible Studies is structured for best consideration of the genre being examined—whether poetry, gospel, history, or narrative. The way we study Esther, a story, differs from how someone might study Paul's Epistle to the Ephesians or the poetry in Song of Songs. So while the studies may have similar elements, no two will be quite the same.

Introduction to
Espresso with Esther

When we think of bad girls of the Bible, the usual culprits such as Jezebel and Rahab come to mind. But Esther isn't usually on the short list. So what was up with that night with the king, anyway?

I was sitting at a sidewalk café two days ago with a couple of my seminary students when one of them asked me that very question. And I had to be honest: I don't think the king whiled away their time together asking Esther what scrolls she'd read lately. From what I've learned from history about him, I'm convinced Esther spent a year preparing for more than the question segment of the beauty pageant (you know…the part where everybody answers "I want world peace").

The woman who had asked me the question said, "That's what I told my mom. And she told me in reply that seminary had ruined me. Esther was her heroine and I shattered her perfect picture."

Yet the way I see it, despite shaky beginnings, Esther does go on to become a great heroine. And in doing so she proves that even a girl with a past—if she has the courage to follow God—can be used to accomplish great things.

Yes, the story of Esther is the story of a beautiful orphan who hides her nationality, becomes queen of the greatest nation on earth at the time, and must decide to risk all to save her people from destruction. She starts out possibly on a compromising note, but she ends up willing to give up her life on behalf of her people.

Esther's story encompasses so much more than that, though. It's also about God. Yet His name is never mentioned.

It's sort of like this . . . . when I was in college, one of my normally-punctual professors burst in the door apologizing that he was late for class. He explained that his wife had given birth that day, and he was in such a frenzy that he had been unable to find his grade book (he needed it to call the roll). He had hunted and hunted for that book, but he just couldn't find it. Then suddenly it had dawned on him where it was—he was holding it in his hand.

I do the same thing when I hunt for my sunglasses and forget they're on top of my head.

Our silent God is a little like that grade book and those sunglasses—sometimes seemingly missing, but always intimately closer than we can imagine.

And Esther reminds us that, though we may want God to show up and speak in a thunderclap or write instructions by forming the clouds into letters, most days we must act in trust and obedience without knowing how everything's going to turn out.

He is sovereign. He is good. We can trust Him.

CONTENTS

WEEK 1 OF 5

Background: Esther 1—10

Scripture: "And the Lord passed by before him and proclaimed: 'The Lord, the Lord,' the compassionate and gracious God, slow to anger, and abounding in loyal love and faithfulness; keeping loyal love for thousands, forgiving iniquity, and transgression and sin. But he by no means leaves the guilty unpunished, visiting the iniquity of the fathers on the children and on the children's children, to the third and fourth generation." (Exodus 34:6–7)

All the girls in my extended family love to get together for movie night when we can watch Sandra Bullock in *Miss Congeniality*. The plot goes something like this: clumsy FBI agent with scary eyebrows and nasty hair undergoes metamorphosis to work undercover as beauty pageant contestant. Subplot: The main character starts out thinking pageants reduce females to their various parts (bad) but ends up believing pageants are positive exercises that emphasize the whole woman—including brains and talent (good).

What do you think of beauty pageants? Do you lean toward the agent's "before" or "after" assessments?

What you think of beauty pageants might have some bearing on how you interpret the first chapter of Esther. Esther is the heroine of the pro-pageant group; Vashti is the heroine of the anti-pageant group.

The Esther group tends to see a great example of the need for wifely submission. Vashti's husband wants her to appear wearing the crown, but Vashti refuses. So she gets what's coming to her: she is deposed and the process of replacing her is set in motion. Bo-o-o, Vashti! Esther later competes in the pageant, wins, and everyone lives happily ever after. Ye-e-ah, Esther!

The Vashti group tends to champion women's rights. They see Vashti's actions as good in refusing to allow her husband to degrade her. Some scholars do believe the king wanted her to appear wearing *only* her crown—a crown which, incidentally, probably signified *his* sovereignty. And historians sometimes point out that, judging by the date in which the event happened, Vashti may have been nine months' pregnant, though others think this was the royals' wedding banquet. The text links the king's demand with an over-abundance of alcohol (1:10) and Ahasuerus later seems to show a hint of remorse (2:1), so the text is tipped a wee bit in Vashti's favor. Some in this camp see Esther as a negative example because she goes along with the status quo.

Frankly, both approaches miss the mark. Esther 1 is not about marriage. Nor is it making a case for feminism. The story is not even about beauty pageants. These subjects are "rabbit trails." The text doesn't focus on any of these aspects, and neither should we. If we take such approaches to "applying" Esther, we miss the point.

Here's why I think it happens. The inductive Bible Study method is a good and popular approach to studying God's word. It emphasizes considering a biblical text first by observing what it says, then interpreting what it means, and finally by making application. This is a particularly fine approach to studying New Testament epistles.

Yet our method must change a bit when we approach Esther and other narratives (stories): we must consider larger blocks of text at one time to find the application the author intended.

If we take the same approach with Esther that we do with the epistles, we might mistakenly "try to apply chapter one" when the entire message doesn't appear unless we look at the entire story from all ten chapters. When studying narratives we need to see the whole story put together before we can see the point or points the author is making. The approach (observation, interpretation, application) is good in both cases; yet what changes is the size of the sections we consider at one time.

Think about what would happen if we drew conclusions about the Three Little Pigs before we knew that the brick house stood despite endless huffing and puffing. Drawing application after the first piggy's house crashes is possible ("wolves can kill you; watch out for them"), but chances are slim that the application we'd take away would be the one actually intended by the author.

A misguided interpretation of Esther, then, is to look at a king giving orders to his wife and her refusal to comply, and then to make any sort of application from that information. The author doesn't tell us whether the king was wrong or whether his wife was wrong. And it's probably for good reason: that's not the point. Such information is background information that lays the groundwork for telling us how Esther got where she did.

So what are the main points of Esther's story? They're not stated in a handy summary. But after we read the entire story we see them: The God of Israel shows loyal love time and again to His covenant people; the Almighty Lord is sovereign in all His dealings; and the Lord of providence kindly cares for His people despite their disobedience. And all that is still true of Him today.

He loves you. He is in control. And He cares about you, no matter what you've done.

MONDAY: HADASSAH'S STORY

1. Pray, asking God to give you understanding and insight. Then read the Book of Esther (below) in one sitting. (It's shorter than a *Reader's Digest* or *Good Housekeeping* short story.)

Esther 1

1:1 The following events happened in the days of Ahasuerus. (I speak of that Ahasuerus who used to rule over a hundred and twenty-seven provinces extending all the way from India to Ethiopia.) **1:2** In those days, as King Ahasuerus sat on his royal throne in Susa the citadel, **1:3** in the third year of his reign he provided a banquet for all his officials and his servants. The army of Persia and Media was present, as well as the nobles and the officials of the provinces.

1:4 He displayed the riches of his royal glory and the splendor of his majestic greatness for a lengthy period of time—a hundred and eighty days, to be exact! **1:5** When those days were completed, the king then provided a seven-day banquet for all the people who were present in Susa the citadel, for those of highest standing to the most lowly. It was held in the court located in the garden of the royal palace. **1:6** The appointments included linen and purple curtains hung by cords of the finest linen and purple wool on silver rings, alabaster columns, gold and silver couches displayed on a surface made of valuable stones of alabaster, mother-of-pearl, and mineral stone. **1:7** Drinks were served in golden containers, all of which differed from one another. Royal wine was available in abundance at the king's expense. **1:8** There were no restrictions on the drinking, for the king had instructed all of his supervisors that they should do as everyone so desired. **1:9** Queen Vashti also gave a banquet for the women in King Ahasuerus' royal palace.

1:10 On the seventh day, as King Ahasuerus was feeling the effects of the wine, he ordered Mehuman, Biztha, Harbona, Bigtha, Abagtha, Zethar, and Carcas, the seven eunuchs who attended him, **1:11** to bring Queen Vashti into the king's presence wearing her royal high turban. He wanted to show the people and the officials her beauty, for she was very attractive. **1:12** But Queen Vashti refused to come at the king's bidding conveyed through the eunuchs. Then the king became extremely angry, and his rage consumed him.

1:13 The king then inquired of the wise men who were discerners of the times—for it was the royal custom to confer with all those who were proficient in laws and legalities. **1:14** Those who were closest to him were Carshena, Shethar, Admatha, Tarshish, Meres, Marsena, and Memucan. These men were the seven officials of Persia and Media who saw the king on a regular basis and had the most prominent offices in the kingdom. **1:15** The king asked, "By law, what should be done to Queen Vashti in light of the fact that she has not obeyed the instructions of King Ahasuerus conveyed through the eunuchs?"

1:16 Memucan then replied to the king and the officials, "The wrong of Queen Vashti is not against the king alone, but against all the officials and all the people who are throughout all the provinces of King Ahasuerus. **1:17** For the matter concerning the queen will spread to all the women, leading them to treat their husbands with contempt, saying, 'When King Ahasuerus gave orders to bring Queen Vashti into his presence, she would not come.' **1:18** And this very day the noble ladies of Persia and Media who have heard the matter concerning the queen will respond in the same way to all the royal officials, and there will be more than enough contempt and anger! **1:19** If the king is so inclined, let a royal edict go forth from him, and let it be written in the laws of Persia and Media that cannot be repealed, that Vashti may not come into the presence of King Ahasuerus, and let the king convey her royalty to another who is more deserving than she. **1:20** And let the king's decision which he will enact be disseminated throughout all his kingdom, vast though it is. Then all the women will give honor to their husbands, from the most prominent to the lowly."

1:21 The matter seemed appropriate to the king and the officials. So the king acted on the advice of Memucan. **1:22** He sent letters throughout all the royal provinces, to each province according to its script and to each people according to its language, that every man should be ruling his family and should be speaking the language of his own people.

Esther 2

2:1 When these things had been accomplished and the rage of King Ahasuerus had diminished, he remembered Vashti and what she had done and what had been decided against her. **2:2** The king's servants who attended him said, "Let a search be conducted in the king's behalf for attractive young women. **2:3** And let the king appoint officers throughout all the provinces of his kingdom to gather all the attractive young women to Susa the citadel, to the harem under the authority of Hegai, the king's eunuch who oversees the women, and let him provide whatever cosmetics they desire. **2:4** Let the young woman whom the king finds most attractive become queen in place of Vashti." This seemed like a good idea to the king, so he acted accordingly.

2:5 Now there happened to be a Jewish man in Susa the citadel whose name was Mordecai. He was the son of Jair, the son of Shimei, the son of Kish, a Benjaminite, **2:6** who had been taken into exile from Jerusalem with the captives who had been carried into exile with Jeconiah king of Judah, whom Nebuchadnezzar king of Babylon had taken into exile. **2:7** Now he was acting as the guardian of Hadassah (that is, Esther), the daughter of his uncle, for neither her father nor her mother was alive. This young woman was very attractive and had a beautiful figure. When her father and mother died, Mordecai had raised her as if she were his own daughter.

2:8 It so happened that when the king's edict and his law became known many young women were taken to Susa the citadel to be placed under the authority of Hegai. Esther also was taken to the royal palace to be under the authority of Hegai, who was overseeing the women. **2:9** This young woman pleased him, and she found favor with him. He quickly provided her with her cosmetics and her rations; he also provided her with the seven special young women who were from the palace. He then transferred her and her young women to the best part of the harem.

2:10 Now Esther had not disclosed her people or her lineage, for Mordecai had instructed her not to do so. **2:11** And day after day Mordecai used to walk back and forth in front of the court of the harem in order to learn how Esther was doing and what might happen to her.

2:12 At the end of the twelve months that were required for the women, when the turn of each young woman arrived to go to King Ahasuerus—for in this way they had to fulfill their time of cosmetic treatment: six months in oil of myrrh, and six months in perfume and various ointments used by women—**2:13** the woman would go to the king in the following way: Whatever she asked for would be provided for her to take with her from the harem to the royal palace. **2:14** In the evening she went, and in the morning she returned to a separate part of the harem, to the authority of Shaashgaz the king's eunuch who was overseeing the concubines. She would not go back to the king unless the king was pleased with her and she was requested by name.

2:15 When it became the turn of Esther daughter of Abihail the uncle of Mordecai (who had raised her as if she were his own daughter) to go to the king, she did not request any thing except for what Hegai the king's eunuch, who was overseer of the women, had recommended. Yet Esther met with the approval of all who saw her. **2:16** Then Esther was taken to King Ahasuerus at his royal residence in the tenth month (that is, the month of Tebeth) in the seventh year of his reign. **2:17** And the king loved Esther more than all the other women, and she met with his loving approval more than all the other young women. So he placed the royal high turban on her head and appointed her queen in place of Vashti. **2:18** Then the king prepared a large banquet for all his officials and his servants— it was actually Esther's banquet. He also set aside a holiday for the provinces, and he provided for offerings at the king's expense.

2:19 Now when the young women were being gathered again, Mordecai was sitting at the king's gate. **2:20** Esther was still not divulging her lineage or her people, just as Mordecai had instructed her. Esther continued to do whatever Mordecai said, just as she had done when he was raising her.

2:21 In those days while Mordecai was sitting at the king's gate, Bigthan and Teresh, two of the king's eunuchs who protected the entrance, got angry and plotted to assassinate King Ahasuerus. **2:22** When Mordecai learned of the conspiracy, he informed Queen Esther, and Esther told the king in Mordecai's behalf. **2:23** The king then had the matter investigated and, finding it to be so, had the two conspirators hanged on a gallows. It was then recorded in the daily chronicles in the king's presence.

Esther 3

3:1 Sometime later King Ahasuerus promoted Haman the son of Hammedatha, the Agagite, exalting him and setting his position above that of all the officials who were with him. **3:2** As a result, all the king's servants who were at the king's gate were bowing and paying homage to Haman, for the king had so commanded. However, Mordecai did not bow, nor did he pay him homage.

3:3 Then the servants of the king who were at the king's gate asked Mordecai, "Why are you violating the king's commandment?" **3:4** And after they had spoken to him day after day without his paying any attention to them, they informed Haman to see whether this attitude on Mordecai's part would be permitted. Furthermore, he had disclosed to them that he was a Jew.

3:5 When Haman saw that Mordecai was not bowing or paying homage to him, he was filled with rage. **3:6** But the thought of striking out against Mordecai alone was repugnant to him, for he had been informed of the identity of Mordecai's people. So Haman sought to destroy all the Jews (that is, the people of Mordecai) who were in all the kingdom of Ahasuerus.

3:7 In the first month (that is, the month of Nisan), in the twelfth year of King Ahasuerus' reign, *pur* (that is, the lot) was cast before Haman in order to determine a day and a month. It turned out to be the twelfth month (that is, the month of Adar).

3:8 Then Haman said to King Ahasuerus, "There is a particular people that is dispersed and spread throughout the inhabitants in all the provinces of your kingdom whose laws differ from those of all other peoples. Furthermore, they do not observe the king's laws. It is not appropriate for the king to provide a haven for them. **3:9** If the king is so inclined, let an edict be issued to destroy them. I will pay ten thousand talents of silver to be conveyed to the king's treasuries for the officials who carry out this business."

3:10 So the king removed his signet ring from his hand and gave it to Haman the son of Hammedatha, the Agagite, who was hostile toward the Jews. **3:11** The king replied to Haman, "Keep your money, and do with those people whatever you wish."

3:12 So the royal scribes were summoned in the first month, on the thirteenth day of the month. Everything Haman commanded was written to the king's satraps and governors who were in every province and to the officials of every people, province by province according to its script and people by people according to its language. In the name of King Ahasuerus it was written and sealed with the king's signet ring. **3:13** Letters were sent by the runners to all the king's provinces stating that they should destroy, kill, and annihilate all the Jews, from youth to elderly, both women and children, on a particular day, namely the thirteenth day of the twelfth month (that is, the month of Adar), and to loot and plunder their possessions. **3:14** A copy of this edict was to be presented as law throughout every province; it was to be made known to all the inhabitants, so that they would be prepared for this day. **3:15** The messengers scurried forth with the king's order. The edict was issued in Susa the citadel. While the king and Haman sat down to drink, the city of Susa was in an uproar!

Esther 4

1 Now when Mordecai became aware of all that had been done, he tore his garments and put on sackcloth and ashes. He went out into the city, crying out in a loud and bitter voice. **4:2** But he went no further than the king's gate, for no one was permitted to enter the king's gate clothed in sackcloth. **4:3** Throughout each and every province where the king's edict and law were announced there was considerable mourning among the Jews, along with fasting, weeping, and sorrow. Sackcloth and ashes were characteristic of many. **4:4** When Esther's female attendants and her eunuchs came and informed her about Mordecai's behavior, the queen was overcome with anguish. Although she sent garments for Mordecai to put on so that he could remove his sackcloth, he would not accept them. **4:5** So Esther called for Hathach, one of the king's eunuchs who had been placed at her service, and instructed him to find out the cause and reason for Mordecai's behavior. **4:6** So Hathach went to Mordecai at the plaza of the city in front of the king's gate. **4:7** Then Mordecai related to him everything that had happened to him, even the specific amount of money that Haman had offered to pay to the king's treasuries for the Jews to be destroyed. **4:8** He also gave him a written copy of the law that had been disseminated in Susa for their destruction so that he could show it to Esther and talk to her about it. He also gave instructions that she should go to the king to implore him and petition him in behalf of her people. **4:9** So Hathach returned and related Mordecai's instructions to Esther.

4:10 Then Esther replied to Hathach with instructions for Mordecai: **4:11** "All the servants of the king and the people of the king's provinces know that there is only one law applicable to any man or woman who comes uninvited to the king in the inner court—that person will be put to death, unless the king extends to him the gold scepter, permitting him to be spared. Now I have not been invited to come to the king for some thirty days!"

4:12 When Esther's reply was conveyed to Mordecai, **4:13** he said to take back this answer to Esther: **4:14** "Don't imagine that because you are part of the king's household you will be the one Jew who will escape. If you keep quiet at this time, liberation and protection for the Jews will appear from another source, while you and your father's household perish. It may very well be that you have achieved royal status for such a time as this!"

4:15 Then Esther sent this reply to Mordecai: **4:16** "Go, assemble all the Jews who are found in Susa and fast in my behalf. Don't eat and don't drink for three days, night or day. My female attendants and I will also fast in the same way. Afterward I will go to the king, even though it violates the law. If I perish, I perish!"

4:17 So Mordecai set out to do everything that Esther had instructed him.

Esther 5

5:1 It so happened that on the third day Esther put on her royal attire and stood in the inner court of the palace, opposite the king's quarters. The king was sitting on his royal throne in the palace, opposite the entrance. **5:2** When the king saw Queen Esther standing in the court, she met with his approval. The king extended to Esther the gold scepter that was in his hand, and Esther approached and touched the end of the scepter.

5:3 The king said to her, "What is on your mind, Queen Esther? What is your request? Even as much as half the kingdom will be given to you!"

5:4 Esther replied, "If the king is so inclined, let the king and

Haman come today to the banquet that I have prepared for him." **5:5** The king replied, "Find Haman quickly so that we can do as Esther requests." So the king and Haman went to the banquet that Esther had prepared. **5:6** While at the banquet of wine, the king said to Esther, "What is your request? It shall be given to you. What is your petition? Ask for as much as half the kingdom, and it shall be done!"

5:7 Esther responded, "My request and my petition is this: **5:8** If I have found favor in the king's sight and if the king is inclined to grant my request and perform my petition, let the king and Haman come tomorrow to the banquet that I will prepare for them. At that time I will do as the king wishes."

Haman Expresses His Hatred of Mordecai

5:9 Now Haman went forth that day pleased and very much encouraged. But when Haman saw Mordecai at the king's gate, and he did not rise nor tremble in his presence, Haman was filled with rage toward Mordecai. **5:10** But Haman restrained himself and went on to his home. He then sent for his friends to join him, along with his wife Zeresh. **5:11** Haman then recounted to them his fabulous wealth, his many sons, and how the king had magnified him and exalted him over the king's other officials and servants. **5:12** Haman said, "Furthermore, Esther the queen invited only me to accompany the king to the banquet that she prepared! And also tomorrow I am invited along with the king. **5:13** Yet all of this fails to satisfy me so long as I have to see Mordecai the Jew sitting at the king's gate."

5:14 Haman's wife Zeresh and all his friends said to him, "Have a gallows seventy-five feet high built, and in the morning tell the king that Mordecai should be hanged on it. Then go satisfied with the king to the banquet." It seemed like a good idea to Haman, so he had the gallows built.

Esther 6

6:1 Throughout that night the king was unable to sleep, so he asked for the book containing the historical records to be brought. As the records were being read in the king's presence, **6:2** it was found written that Mordecai had disclosed that Bigthana and Teresh, two of the king's eunuchs who guarded the entrance, had plotted to assassinate King Ahasuerus.

6:3 The king asked, "What great honor was bestowed on

Mordecai because of this?" The king's attendants who served him responded, "Not a thing was done for him."

6:4 Then the king said, "Who is that in the courtyard?" Now Haman had come to the outer courtyard of the palace to suggest that the king hang Mordecai on the gallows that he had constructed for him. **6:5** The king's attendants said to him, "It is Haman who is standing in the courtyard." The king said, "Let him enter."

6:6 So Haman came in, and the king said to him, "What should be done for the man whom the king wishes to honor?" Haman thought to himself, "Who is it that the king would want to honor more than me?" **6:7** So Haman said to the king, "For the man whom the king wishes to honor, **6:8** let them bring royal attire which the king himself has worn and a horse on which the king himself has ridden—one bearing the royal insignia! **6:9** Then let this clothing and this horse be given to one of the king's noble officials. Let him then clothe the man whom the king wishes to honor, and let him lead him about through the plaza of the city on the horse, calling before him, 'So shall it be done to the man whom the king wishes to honor!'"

6:10 The king then said to Haman, "Go quickly! Take the clothing and the horse, just as you have described, and do as you just indicated to Mordecai the Jew who sits at the king's gate. Don't neglect a single thing of all that you have said."

6:11 So Haman took the clothing and the horse, and he clothed Mordecai. He led him about on the horse throughout the plaza of the city, calling before him, "So shall it be done to the man whom the king wishes to honor!"

6:12 Then Mordecai again sat at the king's gate, while Haman hurried away to his home, mournful and with a veil over his head. **6:13** Haman then related to his wife Zeresh and to all his friends everything that had happened to him. These wise men, along with his wife Zeresh, said to him, "If indeed this Mordecai before whom you have begun to fall is Jewish, you will not be adequate for him. No, you will surely fall before him!"

6:14 While they were still speaking with him, the king's eunuchs arrived. They quickly brought Haman to the banquet that Esther had prepared.

Esther 7

7:1 So the king and Haman came to dine with Queen Esther. **7:2** On the second day of the banquet of wine the king asked Esther,

"What is your request, Queen Esther? It shall be granted to you. And what is your petition? Ask up to half the kingdom, and it shall be done!"

7:3 Queen Esther replied, "If I have met with your approval, O king, and if the king is so inclined, grant me my life as my request, and my people as my petition. **7:4** For we have been sold—both I and my people—to destruction and to slaughter and to annihilation! If we had simply been sold as male and female slaves, I would have remained silent, for such distress would not have been sufficient for troubling the king."

7:5 Then King Ahasuerus responded to Queen Esther, "Who is this individual? Where is this person to be found who is presumptuous enough to act in this way?"

7:6 Esther replied, "The oppressor and enemy is this evil Haman!" Then Haman became terrified in the presence of the king and queen. **7:7** In rage the king arose from the banquet of wine and withdrew to the palace garden. Meanwhile, Haman stood to beg Esther the queen for his life, for he realized that the king had now determined a catastrophic end for him.

7:8 When the king returned from the palace garden to the banquet of wine, Haman was throwing himself down on the couch where Esther was lying. The king exclaimed, "Will he also attempt to rape the queen while I am still in the building!" As these words left the king's mouth, they covered Haman's face. **7:9** Harbona, one of the king's eunuchs, said, "Indeed, there is the gallows that Haman made for Mordecai, who spoke out in the king's behalf. It stands near Haman's home and is seventy-five feet high." The king said, "Hang him on it!" **7:10** So they hanged Haman on the very gallows that he had prepared for Mordecai. The king's rage then abated.

Esther 8

8:1 On that same day King Ahasuerus gave the estate of Haman, that adversary of the Jews, to Queen Esther. Now Mordecai had come before the king, for Esther had revealed how he was related to her. **8:2** The king then removed his signet ring (the very one he had taken back from Haman) and gave it to Mordecai. And Esther designated Mordecai to be in charge of Haman's estate.

8:3 Then Esther again spoke with the king, falling at his feet. She wept and begged him for mercy, that he might nullify the evil of Haman the Agagite which he had intended against the Jews. **8:4**

When the king extended to Esther the gold scepter, she arose and stood before the king.

8:5 She said, "If the king is so inclined and if I have met with his approval and if the matter is agreeable to the king and if I am attractive to him, let an edict be written rescinding those recorded intentions of Haman the son of Hammedatha, the Agagite, which he wrote in order to destroy the Jews who are throughout all the king's provinces. **8:6** For how can I watch the calamity that will befall my people, and how can I watch the destruction of my relatives?"

8:7 King Ahasuerus replied to Queen Esther and to Mordecai the Jew, "Look, I have already given Haman's estate to Esther, and he has been hanged on the gallows because he struck out against the Jews. **8:8** Now you write in the king's name whatever in your opinion is appropriate concerning the Jews and seal it with the king's signet ring. Any decree that is written in the king's name and sealed with the king's signet ring cannot be rescinded.

8:9 The king's scribes were quickly summoned—in the third month (that is, the month of Sivan), on the twenty-third day. They wrote out everything that Mordecai instructed to the Jews and to the satraps and the governors and the officials of the provinces all the way from India to Ethiopia—a hundred and twenty-seven provinces in all—to each province in its own script and to each people in their own language, and to the Jews according to their own script and their own language. **8:10** Mordecai wrote in the name of King Ahasuerus and sealed it with the king's signet ring. He then sent letters by couriers on horses, who rode royal horses that were very swift.

8:11 The king thereby allowed the Jews who were in every city to assemble and to stand up for themselves—to destroy, to kill, and to annihilate any army of whatever people or province that should become their adversaries, including their women and children, and to confiscate their property. **8:12** This was to take place on a certain day throughout all the provinces of King Ahasuerus—namely, on the thirteenth day of the twelfth month (that is, the month of Adar). **8:13** A copy of the edict was to be presented as law throughout each and every province and made known to all peoples, so that the Jews might be prepared on that day to avenge themselves from their enemies.

8:14 The couriers who were riding the royal horses went forth with the king's edict without delay. And the law was presented in Susa the citadel as well.

8:15 Now Mordecai went out from the king's presence in purple and white royal attire, with a large golden crown and a purple linen mantle. The city of Susa shouted with joy. **8:16** For the Jews there was radiant happiness and joyous honor. **8:17** Throughout every province and throughout every city where the king's edict and his law came, the Jews experienced happiness and joy, banquets and holidays. Many of the resident peoples pretended to be Jews, because the fear of the Jews had overcome them.

Esther 9

9:1 In the twelfth month (that is, the month of Adar), on its thirteenth day, the edict of the king and his law were to be executed. It was on this day that the enemies of the Jews had supposed that they would gain power over them. But contrary to expectations, the Jews gained power over their enemies. **9:2** The Jews assembled themselves in their cities throughout all the provinces of King Ahasuerus to strike out against those who were seeking their harm. No one was able to stand before them, for dread of them fell on all the peoples. **9:3** All the officials of the provinces, the satraps, the governors and those who performed the king's business were assisting the Jews, for the dread of Mordecai had fallen on them. **9:4** Mordecai was high ranking in the king's palace, and word about him was spreading throughout all the provinces. His influence continued to become greater and greater.

9:5 The Jews struck all their enemies with the sword, bringing death and destruction, and they did as they pleased with their enemies. **9:6** In Susa the citadel the Jews killed and destroyed five hundred men. **9:7** In addition, they also killed Parshandatha, Dalphon, Aspatha, **9:8** Poratha, Adalia, Aridatha, **9:9** Parmashta, Arisai, Aridai, and Vaizatha, **9:10** the ten sons of Haman son of Hammedatha, the enemy of the Jews. But they did not confiscate their property.

9:11 On that same day the number of those killed in Susa the citadel was brought to the king's attention. **9:12** Then the king said to Queen Esther, "In Susa the citadel the Jews have killed and destroyed five hundred men and the ten sons of Haman! What then have they done in the rest of the king's provinces? What is your request? It shall be given to you. What other petition do you have? It shall be done."

9:13 Esther replied, "If the king is so inclined, let the Jews who are in Susa be permitted to act tomorrow also according to today's law, and let them hang the ten sons of Haman on the gallows."

9:14 So the king issued orders for this to be done. A law was passed in Susa, and the ten sons of Haman were hanged. **9:15** The Jews who were in Susa then assembled on the fourteenth day of the month of Adar, and they killed three hundred men in Susa. But they did not confiscate their property.

9:16 The rest of the Jews who were throughout the provinces of the king assembled in order to stand up for themselves and to have rest from their enemies. They killed seventy-five thousand of their adversaries, but they did not confiscate their property. **9:17** All of this happened on the thirteenth day of the month of Adar. They then rested on the fourteenth day and made it a day for banqueting and happiness.

9:18 But the Jews who were in Susa assembled on the thirteenth and fourteenth days, and rested on the fifteenth, making it a day for banqueting and happiness. **9:19** This is why the Jews who are in the rural country—those who live in rural cities—set aside the fourteenth day of the month of Adar as a holiday for happiness, banqueting, holiday, and sending gifts to one another.

9:20 Mordecai wrote these matters down and sent letters to all the Jews who were throughout all the provinces of King Ahasuerus, both near and far, **9:21** to have them observe the fourteenth and the fifteenth day of the month of Adar each year **9:22** as the time when the Jews gave themselves rest from their enemies—the month when their trouble was turned to happiness and their mourning to a holiday. These were to be days of banqueting, happiness, sending gifts to one another, and providing for the poor.

9:23 So the Jews committed themselves to continue what they had begun to do and to what Mordecai had written to them. **9:24** For Haman the son of Hammedatha, the Agagite, the enemy of all the Jews, had devised plans against the Jews to destroy them. He had cast *pur* (that is, the lot) in order to afflict and destroy them. **9:25** But when the matter came to the king's attention, the king gave written orders that Haman's evil intentions that he had devised against the Jews should fall on his own head. He and his sons were hanged on the gallows. **9:26** For this reason these days are known as *Purim*, after the name of *pur*. **9:27** Therefore, because of the account found in this letter and what they had faced in this regard and what had happened to them, the Jews established as binding on themselves, their descendants, and all who joined their company that they should observe these two days without fail, just as written and at the appropriate time on an annual basis. **9:28** These days were to be remembered and to be celebrated in every generation and in every family, every province, and every city. The Jews were not to fail to observe these days of Purim; the remembrance of them was not to cease among their descendants.

9:29 So Queen Esther, the daughter of Abihail, and Mordecai the Jew wrote with full authority to confirm this second letter about Purim. **9:30** Letters were sent to all the Jews in the hundred and twenty-seven provinces of the empire of Ahasuerus—words of true peace— **9:31** to establish these days of Purim in their proper times, just as Mordecai the Jew and Queen Esther had established, and just as they had established both for themselves and their descendants, matters pertaining to fasting and lamentation. **9:32** Esther's command established these matters of Purim, and the matter was officially recorded.

Esther 10

10:1 King Ahasuerus then imposed forced labor on the land and on the coastlands of the sea. **10:2** Now all the actions carried out under his authority and his great achievements, along with an exact statement concerning the greatness of Mordecai, whom the king promoted, are they not written in the Book of the Chronicles of the Kings of Media and Persia? **10:3** Mordecai the Jew was second only to King Ahasuerus. He was the highest-ranking Jew, and he was admired by his numerous relatives. He worked enthusiastically for the good of his people and was an advocate for the welfare of all his descendants.

2. Write in your own words the gist of the story you've just read:

_____

_____

_____

_____

3. What stands out to you?

_____

_____

_____

_____

4. List a time in your life when at first you could not see God behind the scenes, but later events came together in such a way that you could see His hand at work.

_____

_____

_____

_____

TUESDAY: ISRAEL'S PAST

1. Read the background information below that will help you understand the story of Esther:

Time. The Book of Esther took place in the capital of the Persian Empire at the beginning of King Ahasuerus' reign. Ahasuerus is most likely the king we know in history as Xerxes I. He reigned from approximately 486–465 BC. (That's about one hundred years before Aristotle. The Greek Empire arose after the Persian Empire.) Esther's story is about how a plot to commit genocide against the Jews throughout the vast Persian Empire was thwarted by an orphaned foreigner who rose to the position of queen. This great deliverance of God's people nearly twenty-five hundred years ago is still celebrated each spring in the Jewish feast of Purim. (*Pur* is Hebrew for "lot"—as in casting a lot—probably derived from Akkadian for "stone"; *im* is the Hebrew plural suffix.) The Book of Esther answers the question, "How did the celebration of Purim come about?" We don't know the exact year the book was written, but experts place it somewhere between 450 and 300 BC.

Author. We are not told who wrote the Book of Esther. It's unlikely that Esther herself wrote it, though she would have been the person most familiar with the circumstances. Women—even wealthy, powerful women—in her day usually did not write, though Esther's commands were written by others (see 8:8–10; 9:32). The ancient Jewish historian Josephus along with the church father Clement named Mordecai as the author, but the Jewish *Talmud* attributes it, along with a number of other biblical books, to "men of the Great Synagogue."[1] This refers to a group of one hundred twenty men who are reputed to have lived after the return of the Jewish nation from captivity. The Bible itself does not say who wrote the book or when it was written.

Setting. Before the Great Roman Empire, there was the Greek Empire. And before the Greeks, there were the Medes and the Persians. The Persian Empire was at its height during the roughly two-hundred year period spanning 550 and 330 B.C. Cyrus the Great united the Medes and Persians, serving as the first leader of their combined empire. He captured and took over Babylon (then part of the Babylonian or Chaldean Empire, which had earlier captured Judah, the southern part of the nation of Israel). In the first year of Cyrus's reign, he allowed the people of Judah to return to their homeland, but some, including Mordecai and Esther, stayed behind.

To understand what was happening to Esther's people at this time, it's important to consider a short history of Israel. About 1500 years prior to our story, Abram, though childless, had a promise from God that he would become a great nation (see Gen. 12). God kept His promise, but eventually the descendants of Abraham ended up as slaves in Egypt (see Joseph, King of Dreams or Joseph and the Amazing Technicolor Dreamcoat, or, of course, the latter half of Genesis). About 470 years after Joseph's descendants entered Egypt, Moses led them out of bondage and into the "promised land." (See the animated feature film The Prince of Egypt or, of course, read the Book of Exodus.) Once the people returned to the land, the Lord led them through leaders called judges. This form of leadership as opposed to monarch-rule was God's preference (see The Book of Judges in the Bible). Eventually the people insisted on having kings, so God let them have their way (read 1 and 2 Kings and 1 and 2 Chronicles).

At first the kingdom was united under the reigns of Kings Saul, David, and Solomon. But eventually the nation split into northern (Israel) and southern (Judah) kingdoms. Finally, both north and south were destroyed and their people carried into captivity—the north taken first by Assyria, then the south by Babylon.

---

[1] *Baba Bathra Part I,* chapter V, p. 5, http://www.sacred-texts.com/jud/t07/t0705.htm

As mentioned, in Cyrus's first year he allowed exiled people in Babylonian territory to return to their homelands. This is known as "the first return." For whatever reason, Esther and Mordecai chose to stay in exile.

2. Now that you have a little bit of context for the events, read 2 Chronicles 36.

> The people of the land took Jehoahaz son of Josiah and made him king in his father's place in Jerusalem. **36:2** Jehoahaz was twenty-three years old when he became king, and he reigned three months in Jerusalem. **36:3** The king of Egypt prevented him from ruling in Jerusalem and imposed on the land a special tax of one hundred units of silver and a unit of gold. **36:4** The king of Egypt made Jehoahaz's brother Eliakim king over Judah and Jerusalem, and changed his name to Jehoiakim. Neco seized his brother Jehoahaz and took him to Egypt.

> **36:5** Jehoiakim was twenty-five years old when he became king, and he reigned for eleven years in Jerusalem. He did evil before the Lord his God. **36:6** King Nebuchadnezzar of Babylon attacked him, bound him with bronze chains, and carried him away to Babylon. **36:7** Nebuchadnezzar took some of the items in the Lord's temple to Babylon and put them in his palace there.

> **36:8** The rest of the events of Jehoiakim's reign, including the horrible sins he committed and his shortcomings, are recorded in the Scroll of the Kings of Israel and Judah. His son Jehoiachin replaced him as king.

> **36:9** Jehoiachin was eighteen years old when he became king, and he reigned three months and ten days in Jerusalem. He did evil before the Lord. **36:10** At the beginning of the year King Nebuchadnezzar ordered him to be brought to Babylon, along with the valuable items in the Lord's temple. In his place he made his relative Zedekiah king over Judah and Jerusalem.

> **36:11** Zedekiah was twenty-one years old when he became king, and he ruled for eleven years in Jerusalem. **36:12** He did evil before the Lord his God. He did not humble himself before Jeremiah the prophet, the Lord's spokesman. **36:13** He also rebelled against King Nebuchadnezzar, who had made him vow allegiance in the name of God. He was stubborn and obstinate, and refused to return to the Lord God of Israel. **36:14** All the leaders of the priests and people became more unfaithful and committed the same horrible sins practiced by the nations. They defiled the Lord's temple which he had consecrated in Jerusalem.

36:15 The Lord God of their ancestors continually warned them through his messengers, for he felt compassion for his people and his dwelling place. **36:16** But they mocked God's messengers, despised his warnings, and ridiculed his prophets. Finally the Lord got angry at his people and there was no one who could prevent his judgment. **36:17** He brought against them the king of the Babylonians, who slaughtered their young men in their temple. He did not spare young men or women, or even the old and aging. God handed everyone over to him. **36:18** He carried away to Babylon all the items in God's temple, whether large or small, as well as what was in the treasuries of the Lord's temple and in the treasuries of the king and his officials. **36:19** They burned down the Lord's temple and tore down the wall of Jerusalem. They burned all its fortified buildings and destroyed all its valuable items. **36:20** He deported to Babylon all who escaped the sword. They served him and his sons until the Persian kingdom rose to power. **36:21** This took place to fulfill the Lord's message delivered through Jeremiah. The land experienced its sabbatical years; it remained desolate for seventy years, as prophesied.

36:22 In the first year of the reign of King Cyrus of Persia, in fulfillment of the promise he delivered through Jeremiah, the Lord moved King Cyrus of Persia to issue a written decree throughout his kingdom. **36:23** It read: "This is what King Cyrus of Persia says: 'The Lord God of the heavens has given to me all the kingdoms of the earth. He has appointed me to build for him a temple in Jerusalem in Judah. May the Lord your God energize you who belong to his people, so you may be able to go back there!'"

3. Summarize in your own words the *background* of the Book of Esther.

_____

_____

_____

_____

The Book of Esther takes place between chapters six and seven of Ezra. Below is a summary of Persian leaders and where we find them described in the Bible.

Ruler	Scripture	Description
Cyrus, 559–530 BC	2 Chron. 36; Isa. 44; Dan. 10:1; Ezra 1–6	Babylon's conqueror returned exiled peoples to their homelands. In his first year he permitted Jews to return to Judea.
Cambyses 530–522 BC		
Rule of Magi 522–521 BC		
Darius I 521–486 BC	Ezra 4:5; 5:6–7; Neh. 12:22; Hag. 1:1; Zech. 1:1	Cyrus's successor expanded his earlier decree and ordered completion of the Jerusalem temple at government expense.
Xerxes 486–465 BC	Esther	This expansionist ruler twice invaded Europe and twice was thrown back by the Greeks. He is the likely ruler of Esther.
Artaxerxes 465–425 BC	Ezra 7:1, 21–26; Neh. 2:1–8	Nehemiah served this ruler as cupbearer and was granted the governorship of Judea.[2]

1. Find a comfortable chair, and read Ezra 1—6. What happens?

> **1:1** In the first year of King Cyrus of Persia, in order to fulfill the Lord's message spoken through Jeremiah, the Lord stirred the mind of King Cyrus of Persia. He disseminated a proclamation throughout all his kingdom, announcing in a written edict the following: **1:2** So says King Cyrus of Persia: "'The Lord God of heaven has given me all the kingdoms of the earth. He has instructed me to build a temple for him in Jerusalem, which is in Judah. **1:3** Anyone from his people among you (may his God be with him!) may go up to Jerusalem, which is in Judah, and may build the temple of the Lord God of Israel—he is the

---

[2] Adapted from Lawrence O. Richards, *Bible Readers' Companion* (Colorado Springs: CO, Cook Communications Ministries, 2002), 318, and notes in Herodotus's *The Histories*.

God who is in Jerusalem. **1:4** Let anyone who survives in any of those places where he is a resident foreigner be helped by his neighbors with silver, gold, equipment, and animals, along with voluntary offerings for the temple of God which is in Jerusalem.' "

1:5 Then the leaders of Judah and Benjamin, along with the priests and the Levites—all those whose mind God had stirred—got ready to go up in order to build the temple of the Lord in Jerusalem. **1:6** All their neighbors assisted them with gold, equipment, animals, and expensive gifts, not to mention all the voluntary offerings.

1:7 Then King Cyrus brought out the vessels of the Lord's temple which Nebuchadnezzar had brought from Jerusalem and had displayed in the temple of his gods. **1:8** King Cyrus of Persia entrusted them to Mithredath the treasurer, who counted them out to Sheshbazzar the leader of the Judahite exiles. **1:9** The inventory of these items was as follows: 30 gold basins, 1,000 silver basins, 29 silver utensils,

1:10 30 gold bowls, 410 other silver bowls, and 1,000 other vessels. **1:11** All these gold and silver vessels totaled 5,400. Sheshbazzar brought them all along when the captives were brought up from Babylon to Jerusalem.

Ezra 2

2:1 These are the people of the province who were going up, from the captives of the exile whom King Nebuchadnezzar of Babylon had forced into exile in Babylon. They returned to Jerusalem and Judah, each to his own city. **2:2** They came with Zerubbabel, Jeshua, Nehemiah, Seraiah, Reelaiah, Mordecai, Bilshan, Mispar, Bigvai, Rehum, and Baanah. The number of Israelites was as follows:

2:3 the descendants of Parosh: 2,172;

2:4 the descendants of Shephatiah: 372;

2:5 the descendants of Arah: 775;

2:6 the descendants of Pahath-Moab (from the line of Jeshua and Joab): 2,812;

2:7 the descendants of Elam: 1,254;

2:8 the descendants of Zattu: 945;

2:9 the descendants of Zaccai: 760;

2:10 the descendants of Bani: 642;

2:11 the descendants of Bebai: 623;

2:12 the descendants of Azgad: 1,222;

2:13 the descendants of Adonikam: 666;

2:14 the descendants of Bigvai: 2,056;

2:15 the descendants of Adin: 454;

2:16 the descendants of Ater (through Hezekiah): 98;

2:17 the descendants of Bezai: 323;

2:18 the descendants of Jorah: 112;

2:19 the descendants of Hashum: 223;

2:20 the descendants of Gibbar: 95.

2:21 The men of Bethlehem: 123;

2:22 the men of Netophah: 56;

2:23 the men of Anathoth: 128;

2:24 the men of the family of Azmaveth: 42;

2:25 the men of Kiriath Jearim, Kephirah and Beeroth: 743;

2:26 the men of Ramah and Geba: 621;

2:27 the men of Micmash: 122;

2:28 the men of Bethel and Ai: 223;

2:29 the descendants of Nebo: 52;

2:30 the descendants of Magbish: 156;

2:31 the descendants of the other Elam: 1,254;

2:32 the descendants of Harim: 320;

2:33 the men of Lod, Hadid, and Ono: 725;

2:34 the men of Jericho: 345;

2:35 the descendants of Senaah: 3,630.

2:36 The priests: the descendants of Jedaiah (through the family of Jeshua): 973;

2:37 the descendants of Immer: 1,052;

2:38 the descendants of Pashhur: 1,247;

2:39 the descendants of Harim: 1,017.

2:40 The Levites: the descendants of Jeshua and Kadmiel (through the line of Hodaviah): 74.

2:41 The singers: the descendants of Asaph: 128.

2:42 The gatekeepers: the descendants of Shallum, the descendants of Ater, the descendants of Talmon, the descendants of Akkub, the descendants of Hatita, and the descendants of Shobai: 139.

2:43 The temple servants: the descendants of Ziha, the descendants of Hasupha, the descendants of Tabbaoth, **2:44** the descendants of Keros, the descendants of Siaha, the descendants of Padon, **2:45** the descendants of Lebanah, the descendants of Hagabah, the descendants of Akkub, **2:46** the descendants of Hagab, the descendants of Shalmai, the descendants of Hanan, **2:47** the descendants of Giddel, the descendants of Gahar, the descendants of Reaiah, **2:48** the descendants of Rezin, the descendants of Nekoda, the descendants of Gazzam, **2:49** the descendants of Uzzah, the descendants of Paseah, the descendants of Besai, **2:50** the descendants of Asnah, the descendants of Meunim, the descendants of Nephussim, **2:51** the descendants of Bakbuk, the descendants of Hakupha, the descendants of Harhur, **2:52** the descendants of Bazluth, the descendants of Mehida, the descendants of Harsha, **2:53** the descendants of Barkos, the descendants of Sisera, the descendants of Temah, **2:54** the descendants of Neziah, and the descendants of Hatipha.

2:55 The descendants of the servants of Solomon: the descendants of Sotai, the descendants of Hassophereth, the descendants of Peruda, **2:56** the descendants of Jaala, the descendants of Darkon, the descendants of Giddel, **2:57** the descendants of Shephatiah, the descendants of Hattil, the descendants of Pokereth-Hazzebaim, and the descendants of Ami.

2:58 All the temple servants and the descendants of the servants of Solomon: 392.

2:59 These are the ones that came up from Tel Melah, Tel Harsha, Kerub, Addon, and Immer (although they were unable to certify their family connection or their ancestry, as to whether they really were from Israel):

2:60 the descendants of Delaiah, the descendants of Tobiah, and the descendants of Nekoda: 652.

2:61 And from among the priests: the descendants of Hobaiah, the descendants of Hakkoz, and the descendants of Barzillai (who had taken a wife from the daughters of Barzillai the Gileadite and was called by that name). **2:62** They searched for their records in the genealogical materials, but did not find them. They were therefore excluded from the priesthood. **2:63** The governor instructed them not to eat any of the sacred food until there was a priest who could consult the Urim and Thummim.

2:64 The entire group numbered 42,360, **2:65** not counting their male and female servants, who numbered 7,337. They also had 200 male and female singers **2:66** and 736 horses, 245 mules, **2:67** 435 camels, and 6,720 donkeys. **2:68** When they came to the Lord's temple in Jerusalem, some of the family leaders offered voluntary offerings for the temple of God in order to rebuild it on its site. **2:69** As they were able, they gave to the treasury for this work 61,000 drachmas of gold, 5,000 minas of silver, and 100 priestly robes.

2:70 The priests, the Levites, some of the people, the singers, the gate-keepers, and the temple servants lived in their towns, and all the rest of Israel lived in their towns.

Ezra 3

3:1 When the seventh month arrived and the Israelites were living in their towns, the people assembled in Jerusalem. **3:2** Then Jeshua the son of Jozadak and his priestly colleagues and Zerubbabel son of Shealtiel and his colleagues started to build the altar of the God of Israel so they could offer burnt offerings on it as required by the law of Moses the man of God. **3:3** They established the altar on its foundations, even though they were in terror of the local peoples, and they offered burnt offerings on it to the Lord, both the morning and the evening offerings. **3:4** They observed the Festival of Temporary Shelters as required and offered the proper number of daily burnt offerings according to the requirement for each day. **3:5** Afterward they offered the continual burnt offerings and those for the new moons and those for all the holy assemblies of the Lord and all those that were being voluntarily offered to the Lord. **3:6** From the first day of the seventh month they began to offer burnt offerings to the Lord. But the Lord's temple was not at that time established.

3:7 So they provided money for the masons and carpenters, and food, beverages, and olive oil for the people of Sidon and Tyre, so that they would bring cedar timber from Lebanon to the seaport at Joppa, in accord with the edict of King Cyrus of Persia. **3:8** In the second year after they had come to the temple of God in Jerusalem, in the second month, Zerubbabel the son of Shealtiel and Jeshua the son of Jozadak initiated the work, along with the rest of their associates, the priests and the Levites, and all those who were coming to Jerusalem from the exile. They appointed the Levites who were at least twenty years old to take charge of the work on the Lord's temple. **3:9** So Jeshua appointed both his sons and his relatives, Kadmiel and his sons (the sons of Yehudah), to take charge of the workers in the temple of God, along with the sons of Henadad, their sons, and their relatives the Levites. **3:10** When the builders established the Lord's temple, the priests, ceremonially attired and with their clarions, and the Levites (the sons of Asaph) with their cymbals, stood to praise the Lord according to the instructions left by King David of Israel. **3:11** With antiphonal response they sang, praising and glorifying the Lord: "For he is good; his loving kindness toward Israel is forever." All the people gave a loud shout as they praised the Lord when the temple of the Lord was established. **3:12** Many of the priests, the Levites, and the leaders—older people who had seen with their own eyes the former temple while it was still established—were weeping loudly, and many others raised their voice in a joyous shout. **3:13** People were unable to tell the difference between the sound of joyous shouting and the sound of the people's weeping, for the people were shouting so loudly that the sound was heard a long way off.

Ezra 4

4:1 When the enemies of Judah and Benjamin learned that the former exiles were building a temple for the Lord God of Israel, **4:2** they came to Zerubbabel and the leaders and said to them, "Let us help you build, for like you we seek your God and we have been sacrificing to him from the time of King Esarhaddon of Assyria, who brought us here." **4:3** But Zerubbabel, Jeshua, and the rest of the leaders of Israel said to them, "You have no right to help us build the temple of our God. We will build it by ourselves for the Lord God of Israel, just as King Cyrus, the king of Persia, has commanded us." **4:4** Then the local people began to discourage the people of Judah and to dishearten them from building. **4:5** They were hiring advisers to oppose them, so as to frustrate their plans, throughout the time of King Cyrus of Persia until the reign of King Darius of Persia.

4:6 At the beginning of the reign of Ahasuerus they filed an accusation against the inhabitants of Judah and Jerusalem. **4:7** And in the reign of Artaxerxes, Bishlam, Mithredath, Tabeel, and the rest of their colleagues wrote to King Artaxerxes of Persia. This letter was first written in Aramaic but then translated. [Aramaic:]

4:8 Rehum the commander and Shimshai the scribe wrote a letter concerning Jerusalem to Artaxerxes the king as follows: **4:9** From Rehum the commander, Shimshai the scribe, and the rest of their colleagues—the judges, the rulers, the officials, the secretaries, the Erechites, the Babylonians, the people of Susa (that is, the Elamites), **4:10** and the rest of nations whom the great and noble Ashurbanipal deported and settled in the cities of Samaria and other places in Trans-Euphrates. **4:11** (This is a copy of the letter they sent to him:) "To Artaxerxes the king, from your servants in Trans-Euphrates. **4:12** Now let the king be aware that the Jews who came up to us from you have gone to Jerusalem. They are rebuilding that rebellious and odious city. They are completing its walls and repairing its foundations. **4:13** Let the king also be aware that if this city is built and its walls are completed, no more tax, custom, or toll will be paid, and the royal treasury will suffer loss. **4:14** In light of the fact that we are loyal to the king, and since it does not seem appropriate to us that the king should sustain damage, we are sending the king this information **4:15** so that he may initiate a search of the records of his predecessors and discover in those records that this city is rebellious and injurious to both kings and provinces, producing internal revolts from long ago. It is for this very reason that this city was destroyed. **4:16** We therefore are informing the king that if this city is rebuilt and its walls are completed, you will not retain control of this portion of Trans-Euphrates."

4:17 The king sent the following response: "To Rehum the commander, Shimshai the scribe, and the rest of their colleagues who live in Samaria and other parts of Trans-Euphrates: Greetings! **4:18** The letter you sent to us has been translated and read in my presence. **4:19** So I gave orders, and it was determined that this city from long ago has been engaging in insurrection against kings. It has continually engaged in rebellion and revolt. **4:20** Powerful kings have been over Jerusalem who ruled throughout the entire Trans-Euphrates and who were the beneficiaries of tribute, custom, and toll. **4:21** Now give orders that these men cease their work and that this city not be rebuilt until such time as I so instruct. **4:22** Exercise appropriate caution so that there is no negligence in this matter. Why should danger increase to the point that kings sustain damage?"

4:23 Then, as soon as the copy of the letter from King Artaxerxes was read in the presence of Rehum, Shimshai the scribe, and their colleagues, they proceeded promptly to the Jews in Jerusalem and stopped them with threat of armed force.

4:24 So the work on the temple of God in Jerusalem came to a halt. It remained halted until the second year of the reign of King Darius of Persia.

Ezra 5

5:1 Then the prophets Haggai and Zechariah the son of Iddo prophesied concerning the Jews who were in Judah and Jerusalem in the name of the God of Israel who was over them. **5:2** Then Zerubbabel the son of Shealtiel and Jeshua the son of Jozadak began to rebuild the temple of God in Jerusalem. The prophets of God were with them, supporting them. **5:3** At that time Tattenai governor of Trans-Euphrates, Shethar-Bozenai, and their colleagues came to them and asked, "Who gave you authority to rebuild this temple and to complete this structure?" **5:4** They also asked them, "What are the names of the men who are building this edifice?" **5:5** But God was watching over the elders of Judah, and they were not stopped until a report could be dispatched to Darius and a letter could be sent back concerning this.

5:6 This is a copy of the letter that Tattenai governor of Trans-Euphrates, Shethar-Bozenai, and his colleagues who were the officials of Trans-Euphrates sent to King Darius. **5:7** The report they sent to him was written as follows: "To Darius the king: All greetings! **5:8** Let it be known to the king that we have gone to the province of Judah, to the temple of the great God. It is being built with large stones, and timbers are being placed in the walls. This work is being done with all diligence and is prospering in their hands. **5:9** We inquired of those elders, asking them, 'Who gave you the authority to rebuild this temple and to complete this structure?' **5:10** We also inquired of their names in order to inform you, so that we might write the names of the men who were their leaders. **5:11** They responded to us in the following way: 'We are servants of the God of heaven and earth. We are rebuilding the temple which was previously built many years ago. A great king of Israel built it and completed it. **5:12** But after our ancestors angered the God of heaven, he delivered them into the hands of King Nebuchadnezzar of Babylon, the Chaldean, who destroyed this temple and exiled the people to Babylon. **5:13** But in the first year of King Cyrus of Babylon, King Cyrus enacted a decree to rebuild this temple of God. **5:14** Even the gold and silver vessels of the temple of God that Nebuchadnezzar had taken from the temple in Jerusalem and had brought to the palace of Babylon—even those things King Cyrus brought from the palace of Babylon and presented to a man by the name of Sheshbazzar whom he had appointed as governor. **5:15** He said to him, "Take these vessels and go deposit them in the temple in Jerusalem, and let the house of God be rebuilt in its proper location." **5:16** Then this Sheshbazzar went and laid the foundations of the temple of God in Jerusalem. From that time to the present moment it has been in the process of being rebuilt, although it is not yet finished.'

5:17 "Now if the king is so inclined, let a search be conducted in the royal archives there in Babylon in order to determine whether King Cyrus did in fact issue orders for this temple of God to be rebuilt in Jerusalem. Then let the king send us a decision concerning this matter."

Ezra 6

6:1 So Darius the king issued orders, and they searched in the archives of the treasury which were deposited there in Babylon. **6:2** A scroll was found in the citadel of Ecbatana which is in the province of Media, and it was inscribed as follows: "Memorandum: **6:3** In the first year of his reign, King Cyrus gave orders concerning the temple of God in Jerusalem: 'Let the temple be rebuilt as a place where sacrifices are offered. Let its foundations be raised. Its height is to be ninety feet and its width ninety feet, **6:4** with three layers of large stones and one layer of timber. The expense is to be subsidized by the royal treasury. **6:5** Furthermore, let the gold and silver vessels of the temple of God, which Nebuchadnezzar brought from the temple in Jerusalem and carried to Babylon, be returned and brought to their proper place in the temple in Jerusalem. Let them be deposited in the temple of God.'

6:6 "Now Tattenai governor of Trans-Euphrates, Shethar Bozenai, and their colleagues, the officials of Trans-Euphrates—all of you stay far away from there! **6:7** Leave the work on this temple of God alone. Let the governor of the Jews and the elders of the Jews rebuild this temple of God in its proper place.

6:8 "I also hereby issue orders as to what you are to do with those elders of the Jews in order to rebuild this temple of God. From the royal treasury, from the taxes of Trans-Euphrates the complete costs are to be given to these men, so that there may be no halt. **6:9** Whatever is needed—whether oxen or rams or lambs or burnt offerings for the God of heaven or wheat or salt or wine or oil, as required by the priests who are in Jerusalem—must be given to them daily without any neglect, **6:10** so that they may be offering incense to the God of heaven and may be praying for the good fortune of the king and his family.

6:11 "I hereby give orders that if anyone changes this directive a beam is to be pulled out from his house and he is to be raised up and impaled on it, and his house is to be reduced to a rubbish heap for this indiscretion. **6:12** May God who makes his name to reside there overthrow any king or people who reaches out to cause such change so as to destroy this temple of God in Jerusalem. I, Darius, have given orders. Let them be carried out with precision!"

6:13 Then Tattenai governor of Trans-Euphrates, Shethar-Bozenai, and their colleagues acted accordingly—with precision, just as Darius the king had given instructions. **6:14** The elders of the Jews continued building and prospering, while at the same time Haggai the prophet and Zechariah the son of Iddo continued prophesying.

They built and brought it to completion by the command of the God of Israel and by the command of Cyrus and Darius and Artaxerxes king of Persia. **6:15** They finished this temple on the third day of the month Adar, which is the sixth year of the reign of King Darius.

6:16 The people of Israel—the priests, the Levites, and the rest of the exiles—observed the dedication of this temple of God with joy. **6:17** For the dedication of this temple of God they offered one hundred bulls, two hundred rams, four hundred lambs, and twelve male goats for the sin of all Israel, according to the number of the tribes of Israel. **6:18** They appointed the priests by their divisions and the Levites by their divisions over the worship of God at Jerusalem, in accord with the book of Moses. **6:19** The exiles observed the Passover on the fourteenth day of the first month. **6:20** The priests and the Levites had purified themselves to a man, and they all were ceremonially pure. They sacrificed the Passover lamb for all the exiles, for their colleagues the priests, and for themselves. **6:21** The Israelites who were returning from the exile ate it, along with all those who had joined them in separating themselves from the uncleanness of the nations of the land to seek the Lord God of Israel. **6:22** They observed the Feast of Unleavened Bread for seven days with joy, for the Lord had given them joy and had changed the opinion of the king of Assyria toward them, so that he assisted them in the work on the temple of God, the God of Israel.

2. Now reread the Book of Esther.

3. What, if anything, stood out to you as you read?

_____

_____

_____

THURSDAY: AFTER ESTHER

1. Read Ezra 7—10 and Nehemiah 1:1–2.

7:1 Now after these things had happened, during the reign of King Artaxerxes of Persia, Ezra came up from Babylon. Ezra was the son of Seraiah, who was the son of Azariah, who was the son of

Hilkiah, **7:2** who was the son of Shallum, who was the son of Zadok, who was the son of Ahitub, **7:3** who was the son of Amariah, who was the son of Azariah, who was the son of Meraioth, **7:4** who was the son of Zerahiah, who was the son of Uzzi, who was the son of Bukki, **7:5** who was the son of Abishua, who was the son of Phinehas, who was the son of Eleazar, who was the son of Aaron the chief priest. **7:6** This Ezra is the one who came up from Babylon. He was a scribe who was skilled in the law of Moses which the Lord God of Israel had given. The king supplied him with everything he requested, for the hand of the Lord his God was on him. **7:7** In the seventh year of King Artaxerxes, Ezra brought up to Jerusalem some of the Israelites and some of the priests, the Levites, the attendants, the gatekeepers, and the temple servants in the seventh year of King Artaxerxes. **7:8** He entered Jerusalem in the fifth month of the seventh year of the king. **7:9** On the first day of the first month he had determined the ascent from Babylon, and on the first day of the fifth month he arrived at Jerusalem, for the good hand of his God was on him. **7:10** Now Ezra had given himself to the study of the law of the Lord, to its observance, and to teaching its statutes and judgments in Israel.

7:11 What follows is a copy of the letter that King Artaxerxes gave to Ezra the priestly scribe. Ezra was a scribe in matters pertaining to the commandments of the Lord and his statutes over Israel:

7:12 "Artaxerxes, king of kings, to Ezra the priest, a scribe of the perfect law of the God of heaven. **7:13** I have now issued a decree that anyone in my kingdom from the people of Israel—even the priests and Levites—who wishes to do so may go up with you to Jerusalem. **7:14** You are authorized by the king and his seven advisers to inquire concerning Judah and Jerusalem, according to the law of your God which is in your possession, **7:15** and to bring silver and gold which the king and his advisers have freely contributed to the God of Israel, who resides in Jerusalem, **7:16** along with all the silver and gold that you may collect throughout all the province of Babylon and the contributions of the people and the priests for the temple of their God which is in Jerusalem. **7:17** With this money you should be sure to purchase bulls, rams, and lambs, along with the appropriate meal offerings and libations. You should bring them to the altar of the temple of your God which is in Jerusalem. **7:18** You may do whatever seems appropriate to you and your colleagues with the rest of the silver and the gold, in keeping with the will of your God. **7:19** Deliver to the God of Jerusalem the vessels that are given to you for the service of the temple of your God. **7:20** The rest of the needs for the temple of your God that you may have to supply, you may do so from the royal treasury.

7:21 "I, Artaxerxes the king, hereby issue orders to all the treasurers of Trans-Euphrates, that you precisely execute all that Ezra the priestly scribe of the law of the God of heaven may request of you— **7:22** up to 100 talents of silver, 100 cors of wheat, 100 baths of wine, 100 baths of olive oil, and unlimited salt. **7:23** Everything that the God of heaven has required should be precisely done for the temple of the God of heaven. Why should there be wrath against the empire of the king and his sons? **7:24** Furthermore, be aware of the fact that you have no authority to impose tax, tribute, or toll on any of the priests, the Levites, the musicians, the doorkeepers, the temple servants, or the attendants at the temple of this God.

7:25 "Now you, Ezra, in keeping with the wisdom of your God which you possess, appoint judges and court officials who can arbitrate cases on behalf of all the people who are in Trans-Euphrates who know the laws of your God. Those who do not know this law should be taught. **7:26** Everyone who does not observe both the law of your God and the law of the king will be completely liable to the appropriate penalty, whether by death or banishment or confiscation of property or detainment in prison."

7:27 Blessed be the Lord God of our fathers, who so moved in the heart of the king to so honor the temple of the Lord which is in Jerusalem! **7:28** He has also conferred his favor on me before the king, his advisers, and all the influential leaders of the king. I gained strength as the hand of the Lord my God was on me, and I gathered leaders from Israel to go up with me.

Ezra 8

8:1 These are the leaders and those enrolled with them by genealogy, who were coming up with me from Babylon during the reign of King Artaxerxes:

8:2 from the descendants of Phinehas, Gershom; from the descendants of Ithamar, Daniel; from the descendants of David, Hattush **8:3** the son of Shecaniah; from the descendants of Parosh, Zechariah, and with him were enrolled by genealogy 150 men;

8:4 from the descendants of Pahath-Moab, Eliehoenai son of Zerahiah, and with him 200 men;

8:5 from the descendants of Zattu, Shecaniah son of Jahaziel, and with him 300 men;

8:6 from the descendants of Adin, Ebed son of Jonathan, and with him 50 men;

8:7 from the descendants of Elam, Jeshaiah son of Athaliah, and with him 70 men;

8:8 from the descendants of Shephatiah, Zebadiah son of Michael, and with him 80 men;

8:9 from the descendants of Joab, Obadiah son of Jehiel, and with him 218 men;

8:10 from the descendants of Bani, Shelomith son of Josiphiah, and with him 160 men;

8:11 from the descendants of Bebai, Zechariah son of Bebai, and with him 28 men;

8:12 from the descendants of Azgad, Johanan son of Hakkatan, and with him 110 men;

8:13 from the descendants of Adonikam there were the latter ones. Their names were Eliphelet, Jeuel, and Shemaiah, and with them 60 men;

8:14 from the descendants of Bigvai, Uthai, and Zaccur, and with them 70 men.

8:15 I had them assemble at the canal that flows toward Ahava, and we camped there for three days. I observed that the people and the priests were present, but I found no Levites there. **8:16** So I sent for Eliezer, Ariel, Shemaiah, Elnathan, Jarib, Elnathan, Nathan, Zechariah, and Meshullam, who were leaders, and Joiarib and Elnathan, who were teachers. **8:17** I sent them to Iddo, who was the leader in the place called Casiphia. I told them what to say to Iddo and his brethren, who were the temple servants in Casiphia, so they would bring us attendants for the temple of our God.

8:18 Due to the fact that the good hand of our God was on us, they brought us a skilled man, from the descendants of Mahli the son of Levi son of Israel. This Sherebiah came, along with his sons and relatives, 18 men, **8:19** and Hashabiah, along with Jeshaiah from the descendants of Merari, with his brothers and their sons, 20 men, **8:20** and some of the temple servants that David and his officials had established for the work of the Levites—220 of them. They were all designated by name.

8:21 I called for a fast there by the Ahava Canal, so that we might humble ourselves before our God and seek from him a safe journey for us, our children, and all our property. **8:22** I was embarrassed to request soldiers and horsemen from the king to protect us from the enemy along the way, because we had said to the king, "The good hand of our God is on everyone who is seeking him, but his great anger is on everyone who forsakes him." **8:23** So we fasted and prayed to our God about this, and he answered us.

8:24 Then I set apart twelve of the leading priests, together with Sherebiah, Hashabiah, and ten of their brothers, **8:25** and I weighed out to them the silver, the gold, and the vessels intended for the temple of our God—items that the king, his advisers, his officials, and all Israel who were present had contributed. **8:26** I weighed out to them 650 talents of silver, silver vessels worth 100 talents, 100 talents of gold, **8:27** 20 gold bowls worth 1,000 darics, and two exquisite vessels of gleaming bronze, as valuable as gold. **8:28** Then I said to them, "You are holy to the Lord, just as these vessels are holy. The silver and the gold are a voluntary offering to the Lord, the God of your fathers. **8:29** Be careful with them and protect them, until you weigh them out before the head priests and the Levites and the family leaders of Israel in Jerusalem, in the storerooms of the temple of the Lord."

8:30 Then the priests and the Levites took charge of the silver, the gold, and the vessels that had been weighed out, to transport them to Jerusalem to the temple of our God.

8:31 On the twelfth day of the first month we began traveling from the Ahava Canal to go to Jerusalem. The hand of our God was on us, and he delivered us from our enemy and from bandits along the way. **8:32** So we came to Jerusalem, and we stayed there for three days. **8:33** On the fourth day we weighed out the silver, the gold, and the vessels in the house of our God into the care of Meremoth son of Uriah, the priest, and Eleazar son of Phinehas, who were accompanied by Jozabad son of Jeshua and Noadiah son of Binnui, who were Levites. **8:34** Everything was verified by number and by weight, and the total weight was written down at that time.

8:35 The exiles who were returning from the captivity offered burnt offerings to the God of Israel—twelve bulls for all Israel, ninety-six rams, seventy-seven male lambs, along with twelve male goats as a sin offering. All this was a burnt offering to the Lord. **8:36** Then they presented the decrees of the king to the king's satraps and to the governors of Trans-Euphrates, who gave help to the people and to the temple of God.

Ezra 9

9:1 Now when these things had been completed, the leaders approached me and said, "The people of Israel, the priests, and the Levites have not separated themselves from the local residents who practice detestable things similar to those of the Canaanites, the Hittites, the Perizzites, the Jebusites, the Ammonites, the Moabites, the Egyptians, and the Amorites. **9:2** Indeed, they have taken some of their daughters as wives for themselves and for their sons and have intermingled the holy seed with the local residents. Worse still, the leaders and the officials have been at the forefront of all of this!"

9:3 When I heard this account, I tore my tunic and my robe and ripped out some of the hair of my head and beard. Then I sat down, quite devastated. **9:4** Everyone who held the words of the God of Israel in awe gathered around me because of the unfaithful acts of the people of the exile. Devastated, I continued to sit there until the evening offering.

9:5 At the time of the evening offering I got up from my self-abasement, with my torn tunic and robe, and then dropped to my knees and spread my hands to the Lord my God. **9:6** I prayed, "O my God, I am ashamed and embarrassed, my God, to lift my face to you. For our iniquities have climbed higher than our head, and our guilt extends to the heavens. **9:7** From the days of our fathers until this very day our guilt has been great. Because of our iniquities we, along with our kings and priests, have been delivered over by the local kings to sword, captivity, plunder, and embarrassment—right up to the present time.

9:8 "But now briefly we have received mercy from the Lord our God, in that he has left us a remnant and has given us a secure position in his holy place. Thus our God has enlightened our eyes and has given us a little relief in our time of servitude. **9:9** Although we are slaves, our God has not abandoned us in our servitude. He has extended kindness to us in the sight of the kings of Persia, in that he has revived us to restore the temple of our God and to raise up its ruins and to give us a protective wall in Judah and Jerusalem.

9:10 "And now what are we able to say after this, our God? For we have forsaken your commandments **9:11** which you commanded us through your servants the prophets with the words: 'The land that you are entering to possess is a land defiled by the impurities of the local residents. With their abominations they have filled it from one end to the other with their filthiness. **9:12** Therefore do not give your daughters in marriage to their sons, and do not take their daughters in marriage for your sons. Do not ever seek their peace or welfare, so that you may be strong and may eat the good of the land and may leave it as an inheritance for your sons forever.'

9:13 "Everything that has happened to us has come about because of our wicked actions and our great guilt. Even so, our God, you have exercised restraint toward our iniquities and have given us a remnant such as this. **9:14** Shall we once again break your commandments and intermarry with these abominable peoples? Would you not be so angered by us as to wipe us out, with no survivor or remnant? **9:15** O Lord God of Israel, you are righteous, for we are left as a remnant this day. Indeed, we stand before you in our guilt. However, because of this guilt no one can really stand before you."

Ezra 10

10:1 While Ezra was praying and confessing, weeping and throwing himself to the ground before the temple of God, a very large crowd of Israelites—men, women, and children alike—gathered around him. The people wept loudly. **10:2** Then Shecaniah son of Jehiel, from the descendants of Elam, addressed Ezra: "We have been unfaithful to our God by marrying foreign women from the local peoples. Nonetheless, there is still hope for Israel in this regard. **10:3** Therefore let us enact a covenant with our God to send away all these women and their offspring, in keeping with the counsel of my lord and of those who have regard for the commandments of our God. And let it be done according to the law. **10:4** Get up, for this matter concerns you. We are with you, so be strong and act decisively."

10:5 So Ezra got up and made the leading priests and Levites and all Israel take an oath to carry out this plan. And they all took a solemn oath. **10:6** Then Ezra got up from before the temple of God and went to the room of Jehohanan son of Eliashib. While he stayed there, he did not eat food, nor did he drink water, for he was in mourning over the infidelity of the exiles.

10:7 A proclamation was circulated throughout Judah and Jerusalem that all the exiles were to be assembled in Jerusalem. **10:8** Everyone who did not come within three days would thereby forfeit all his property, in keeping with the counsel of the officials and the elders. Furthermore, he himself would be excluded from the assembly of the exiles.

10:9 All the men of Judah and Benjamin were gathered in Jerusalem within the three days. (It was in the ninth month, on the twentieth day of that month.) All the people sat in the square at the temple of God, trembling because of this matter and because of the rains.

10:10 Then Ezra the priest stood up and said to them, "You have behaved in an unfaithful manner by taking foreign wives! This has contributed to the guilt of Israel. **10:11** Now give praise to the

Lord God of your fathers, and do his will. Separate yourselves from the local residents and from these foreign wives."

10:12 All the assembly replied in a loud voice: "We will do just as you have said! **10:13** However, the people are numerous and it is the rainy season. We are unable to stand here outside. Furthermore, this business cannot be resolved in a day or two, for we have sinned greatly in this matter. **10:14** Let our leaders take steps on behalf of all the assembly. Let all those in our towns who have married foreign women come at an appointed time, and with them the elders of each town and its judges, until the hot anger of our God is turned away from us in this matter."

10:15 Only Jonathan son of Asahel and Jahzeiah son of Tikvah were against this, assisted by Meshullam and Shabbethai the Levite. **10:16** So the exiles proceeded accordingly. Ezra the priest separated out by name men who were leaders in their family groups. They sat down to consider this matter on the first day of the tenth month, **10:17** and on the first day of the first month they finished considering all the men who had married foreign wives.

10:18 It was determined that from the descendants of the priests, the following had taken foreign wives: from the descendants of Jeshua son of Jozadak, and his brothers: Maaseiah, Eliezer, Jarib, and Gedaliah. **10:19** (They gave their word to send away their wives; their guilt offering was a ram from the flock for their guilt.)

10:20 From the descendants of Immer: Hanani and Zebadiah.

10:21 From the descendants of Harim: Maaseiah, Elijah, Shemaiah, Jehiel, and Uzziah.

10:22 From the descendants of Pashhur: Elioenai, Maaseiah, Ishmael, Nethanel, Jozabad, and Elasah.

10:23 From the Levites: Jozabad, Shimei, Kelaiah (also known as Kelita), Pethahiah, Judah, and Eliezer.

10:24 From the singers: Eliashib. From the gatekeepers: Shallum, Telem, and Uri.

10:25 From the Israelites: from the descendants of Parosh: Ramiah, Izziah, Malkijah, Mijamin, Eleazar, Malkijah, and Benaiah.

10:26 From the descendants of Elam: Mattaniah, Zechariah, Jehiel, Abdi, Jeremoth, and Elijah.

10:27 From the descendants of Zattu: Elioenai, Eliashib, Mattaniah, Jeremoth, Zabad, and Aziza.

10:28 From the descendants of Bebai: Jehohanan, Hananiah, Zabbai, and Athlai.

10:29 From the descendants of Bani: Meshullam, Malluch, Adaiah, Jashub, Sheal, and Jeremoth.

10:30 From the descendants of Pahath-Moab: Adna, Kelal, Benaiah, Maaseiah, Mattaniah, Bezalel, Binnui, and Manasseh.

10:31 From the descendants of Harim: Eliezer, Ishijah, Malkijah, Shemaiah, Shimeon, **10:32** Benjamin, Malluch, and Shemariah.

10:33 From the descendants of Hashum: Mattenai, Mattattah, Zabad, Eliphelet, Jeremai, Manasseh, and Shimei.

10:34 From the descendants of Bani: Maadai, Amram, Uel, **10:35** Benaiah, Bedeiah, Keluhi, **10:36** Vaniah, Meremoth, Eliashib, **10:37** Mattaniah, Mattenai, and Jaasu.

10:38 From the descendants of Binnui: Shimei, **10:39** Shelemiah, Nathan, Adaiah, **10:40** Machnadebai, Shashai, Sharai, **10:41** Azarel, Shelemiah, Shemariah, **10:42** Shallum, Amariah, and Joseph.

10:43 From the descendants of Nebo: Jeiel, Mattithiah, Zabad, Zebina, Jaddai, Joel, and Benaiah.

10:44 All these had taken foreign wives, and some of them also had children by these women.

Nehemiah 1:1 These are words of Nehemiah son of Hacaliah: It so happened that in the month of Kislev, in the twentieth year, I was in Susa the citadel. **1:2** Hanani, who was one of my relatives, along with some of the men from Judah, came to me, and I asked them about the fugitive Jews who remained from the exile and about Jerusalem.

2. Describe what you perceive the world to be like at the time Esther was written.

_____

_____

3. How would you describe the spiritual state of God's people during the era when Ezra and Esther lived?

_____

_____

_____

1. The Persian Empire was enormous. Where was that Empire located, according to Esther 1:1?

The Empire. King Xerxes ruled the most powerful kingdom in

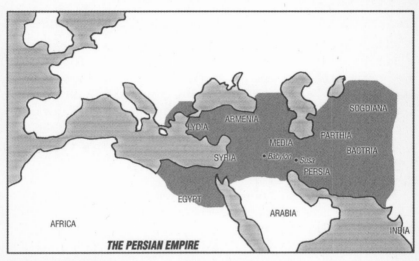

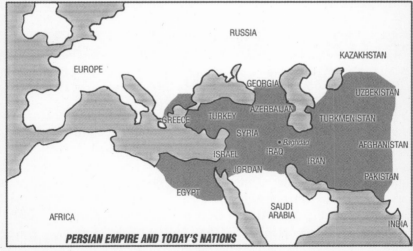

Drawings: Keith Yates

the world at that time he lived. The Persian Empire covered a huge territory which included the upper Nile in Africa through Ethiopia and over to India. (This includes parts of modern-day Albania, Bulgaria, Turkey, Syria, Israel, Jordan, Egypt, Iran, Iraq, Georgia, Azerbaijan, Uzbekistan, Turkmenistan, Afghanistan, and Pakistan.)

2. Locate Susa on the map on page 39 (top).

3. How does Nehemiah describe Susa (Nehemiah 1:1)?

The City. The city of *Susa* (Hebrew: *Shushan*) was one of several capitals of the Persian Empire, the best known being Babylon. Susa was primarily the winter palace. It was too hot to inhabit in the summer, when it is said that reptiles merely crossing the road would die from the heat. Today Susa is nothing but ruins, but for centuries it was one of the oldest cities in the world. A fire destroyed it after the reign of Xerxes, and during the Persian Gulf War its ruins were further destroyed.

4. Study the maps and observe the vast region over which Xerxes reigned. How many modern-day countries can you count that were within the Persian Empire?

SATURDAY: WHAT'S IN A NAME?

Scripture: "Esther did not make known her people or her kindred, for Mordecai had instructed her that she should not make them known." (Esth. 2:10)

After ten years of infertility, my husband and I rejoiced over the successful adoption of our daughter—a beautiful, eight-month-old. Because she was not a newborn, her birth parents had already named her. But as a way of making her a member of our family, we gave her a new name—Alexandra Glahn. My name, Sandra, is a shorter form of hers. We decided that if we couldn't give her a part of our physical selves, we could give her first and last names that said she was ours.

Names are important. And to God's people in biblical times, names were a big deal. Case in point: the one guy *not* mentioned by name in the book of Ruth is the guy who *should* have taken care of Ruth, but who didn't. In the curtain call at the end we read a list of names like Perez and Hezron, Ram and Amminadab, Nahshon and Salmon on down, but there's not one word about the guy who refused to take Ruth as his wife because he wanted to secure for himself a better future.

It's not that names are unimportant now. Nobody today wants to be called Stinker or Shrimp. When we were kids, my siblings and I found Ima Hogg in the phone book and laughed ourselves silly. And we used to laugh about the kid in our school named Harry Butts. (We were wicked!)

Esther lived in a time when the Persian king, Khshayarsha, reigned. He is better known to us by his Greek name, Xerxes. This whole thing about people having more than one name is not that unusual even today, if we think about it. Our daughter's name is Alexandra, but to our Russian friends she is Sasha—or the more endearing "Sashenka." Her "Southern girl" nickname, by which she is known to a neighbor and to us, is "Lucy Belle." The names may sound nothing alike, but then the equivalent for William in Spanish is Guerillmo. Go figure.

But what about Esther? The name Esther may sound lovely, but it really wasn't all that great at the time, if we think about it. Of course, now that we know Esther's whole story, the name may remind us of God's providence—about how, during a dark time in the history of His people, He kept His promises and was still in control. But the young orphan girl going by a new name—a Persian name—was not exactly a good thing. (As she grew, her cousin insisted that she withhold information about her nationality and family background; see Esther 2:10.)

The name "Esther" means "star," and it probably comes from the same root word as "Ishtar," the Babylonian goddess of love. Esther's Hebrew name was actually Hadassah, which means myrtle—like the beautiful, sweet-smelling shrub with white leaves. The Jewish people still sometimes carry myrtle branches as they march in procession during the Feast of Booths or Succoth, more commonly known to us as the Feast of Tabernacles.

It was not all that unusual to have a "secular" name and a "Jewish" name. Daniel did. So did Shadrach, Meshach, and Abednego (not their Hebrew names). But Esther's "pagan" name is rather symbolic. Unlike Daniel, who refused to defile himself with the king's meat while living in a pagan culture, Esther ate unclean food—a practice forbidden in God's law (see Lev. 11:46). She may have given up her virginity to a man who was not her husband as she competed in the beauty contest. And after she "won," she married the king, a pagan—also disallowed (Deut. 7:1–4). No, Esther was not exactly a pristine, God-fearing citizen—at least, not until rather late in the story.

Now, when we run down the list of bad girls in the Bible, we don't usually throw Esther in with Bathsheba and Jezebel. Yet she was actually a girl with a history, if we think about it. Nevertheless, in a book in which the name of God is never mentioned and prayers are never said, we get the clear message that God has absolute power over individuals and history. And in this case He does so through a girl who has gone her own way.

And you know what? We're not all that much different from that girl.

Imagine a video screen projecting every moment of our inner thoughts and outward actions in front of a group of holy people. Throw in scenes of impatience in grocery lines; the gestures in traffic—whether mental or actual; the petty things said; the less-than-stellar dating life; the movies; the magazines; the Internet sites; the pride when we put down others to elevate ourselves. Add to that the lies we told even ourselves, taken in by the deceitfulness of sin. For some there's also carousing, lack of regard for others' property, drunk driving, drug abuse, abortions, and illicit relationships. (Interestingly, the last few aren't even on the list of vices or things God hates. We tend to think of them as the absolute worst, but if we're honest, we know Jesus had a lot less patience with the Pharisees than with the hooker who washed His feet with her perfume.)

No, we don't have to endure the embarrassment of full exposure—which is a merciful thing. Instead, when God sees the life of the Christian, He sees the righteousness of Christ. That's how He views us. When we confess, the record of them disappears. And that's grace.

Like Esther, we are imperfect, full of failures and flaws. Yet God still uses us, not because we're good, but because *He* is.

When I was a new Christian, people warned me that if I failed to follow the Lord, He couldn't use me. That was completely untrue. The truth was that if I didn't keep walking with Him, I would lose out on the peace, joy, and blessing that come with obedience. God has used lots of disobedient people and He still does. He can use anything—from a talking donkey to rocks crying out, if need be.

Think back through some of the characters in scripture. There was the rebellious missionary (Jonah), the guy with the sexual addiction (Samson), the call girl in Jericho (Rahab) and a whole lot of other people who weren't exactly "hall of perfection" material. Now, think about Hebrews 11, often called "the faith chapter." It could just as easily be titled "the mess-up chapter" with the exception of Abel and a short list of others. The grand heroes such as Mary, Enoch, and Daniel aren't found there either. Instead we see names like Abraham and Sarah (Abe lied; Sarah laughed), Jacob (the deceiver), and Jephthah, who sacrificed his own daughter! This is not the *perfection* chapter; it's the *faith* chapter.

In Esther we find an ordinary girl who wants to keep a low profile about her nationality, but who ends up cooperating with God to use the very thing she wants to hide to save a nation. During her period of disobedience, God weaves the threads of her wrongdoing to set up circumstances that will glorify Him—circumstances that He brings to fruition once she does the right thing.

Only God can use even our sins for His good, and the Book of Esther is a book about such a reversal. Talk about God's providence! It's also about grace. It reminds us that God can use anybody, anytime, often choosing the most unlikely, unworthy people—people like you and like me.

What have you done that you regret? Offer Him your past and your present, your weaknesses and your gifts, your failures and your successes. Express your willingness for Him to use it all. Don't lose out on the peace, joy, and blessing that come with obedience.

Prayer: *O God of great reversals, thank You for Your grace! You poured out Your favor on me, even when I was still Your enemy lost in sin. All that I am and all that I have and all that I have been, I offer to You to use for Your glory. Thank You that You are sovereign over everything and that you can use anything anytime. Grant me an obedient heart to follow You fully. I pray these things in the name of the Son whom You sent in Your grace, Amen.*

For Memorization: "Then the LORD passed by in front of him and proclaimed, 'The LORD, the LORD God, compassionate and gracious, slow to anger, and abounding in lovingkindness and truth; who keeps lovingkindness for thousands, who forgives iniquity, transgression and sin; yet He will by no means leave the guilty unpunished, visiting the iniquity of fathers on the children and on the grandchildren to the third and fourth generations." (Exod. 34:6–7 NASB)

Week 2 of 5

Meet the Characters: Esther 1–10

Scripture: *"Don't imagine that because you are part of the king's household you will be the one Jew who will escape. If you keep quiet at this time, liberation and protection for the Jews will appear from another source, while you and your father's household perish. It may very well be that you have achieved royal status for such a time as this!"* (Esther: 4:14)

When you were a child, did you ever spin around in a long dress pretending to be Cinderella? Perhaps you watched *Cinderella* on TV or video. Was it a cartoon version? Maybe a parent or sibling read it to you. Or perhaps you saw Rogers and Hammerstein's 1965 production starring Lesley Ann Warren. Maybe you watched the 1997 show with Brandy, Paola Montalban, and Whitney Houston. If you're a big Cinderella fan, perhaps you saw and read all of these and more.

What about *My Fair Lady*—did you ever imitate Eliza Dolittle singing about the rain in Spain (or the rine in spine)? Did you mentally protest against Henry Higgins when he asked "Why can't a woman be more like a man?"?

Many cultures have their rags-to-riches stories like *Cinderella* and *My Fair Lady.* The details differ, but the general plotline is the same: a poor, plain girl of questionable pedigree rises from poverty to become rich and beautiful, perhaps even the queen of a vast empire.

The Book of Esther is like a Hebrew Cinderella story. Yet some significant differences set this drama apart from fictional stories such as those mentioned above. For one thing, Esther's story actually happened. The book begins with the same formula that introduces the historical books of Joshua, Judges, Ruth, 1 Samuel, 2 Samuel, Ezekiel, and Jonah. We are supposed to read Esther as fact, not fancy.

Another key difference is that in Esther, the villain (Haman) is far worse than any evil stepmother or chauvinistic linguistics coach. Haman is out to commit genocide, and the king approves his plan without hesitation.

Yet there's an even more significant difference: the main character in this Cinderella story is someone other than the woman at the center of the drama. In fact this story's main character is never explicitly mentioned by name, nor does He appear. An accurate playbill for this drama would have to have an empty space next to the photo of the one playing the lead. He is invisible, yet we trace His hand through every turn in the plot as the seeming coincidences add up.

William Temple, the ninety-eighth archbishop of Canterbury, was known to have said, "When I pray, coincidences happen; and when I don't pray, they don't happen." The author of the Book of Esther stacks together a long string of "coincidences," while never mentioning anything religious such as the temple, prayer, or even God's name. Yet readers without being told know better than to think all the events in the book merely happened due to chance. We are left instead with one conclusion: The only way all these "coincidences" could have happened is if God directed every last detail.

Consider some of the "coincidences" in Esther's story:

- The king wants his wife to appear, which just happens to set in motion events that will lead to the survival of an entire people group.
- The queen refuses, which just happens to provide the opportunity for Esther to become queen.
- Esther just happens to be beautiful enough to enter (and win) the king's beauty contest.
- Esther just happens to be received favorably, both by the eunuch over the harem and by the king himself.

- Mordecai just happens to be in a position in the palace that allows him both access to Esther and to overhear a plot to kill the king.
- Mordecai's revelation of the plot is recorded in the king's annals (which just happen to be read on the most opportune night some *years later*).
- The dice or "lots" thrown to determine when the Jews are to be killed just happen to indicate the twelfth month, allowing eleven months for the Jews to seek a means of deliverance.
- Esther's unexplained delay in having a second banquet just happens to allow the king a chance to have the insomnia that will motivate him to listen to his chronicles. The section read to him just happens to be the part about how Mordecai saved his life.
- Haman just happens to arrive at the palace with Mordecai on his mind at the very moment when the king is thinking about how to honor Mordecai.
- The very "gallows" (or pole) Haman installed for having Mordecai impaled (they would "spike" people after killing them) just happens to be the means of Haman's own destruction.
- The king's entry into Esther's room at the exact moment when Haman falls on her couch just happens to make him misinterpret events, resulting in Haman's death.
- Not one Jew is listed as killed while 75,800 of their enemies just happen to be destroyed—on the very day when the Jews were to face destruction.

This Cinderella story has ramifications that far exceed an "if the shoe fits" scenario. Much more is at stake than a glass slipper and love that ends "happily ever after." Ultimately, Esther just happens to be in the right place at the right time and of the right nationality to intervene for hundreds of thousands if not millions of people and save them from certain genocide. God uses Esther to make a way, to keep His promise, to triumph over evil in one grand reversal.

And He is still sovereign over every event of our lives today.

MONDAY: MEET AHASUERUS

1. Read the reading for the week, which is Esther 1:1—2:10. Underline any words that stand out, or write any observations that come to mind as you reread the text.

Esther 1

1:1 The following events happened in the days of Ahasuerus. (I speak of that Ahasuerus who used to rule over a hundred and twenty-seven provinces extending all the way from India to Ethiopia.) **1:2** In those days, as King Ahasuerus sat on his royal throne in Susa the citadel, **1:3** in the third year of his reign he provided a banquet for all his officials and his servants. The army of Persia and Media was present, as well as the nobles and the officials of the provinces.

1:4 He displayed the riches of his royal glory and the splendor of his majestic greatness for a lengthy period of time—a hundred and eighty days, to be exact! **1:5** When those days were completed, the king then provided a seven-day banquet for all the people who were present in Susa the citadel, for those of highest standing to the most lowly. It was held in the court located in the garden of the royal palace. **1:6** The appointments included linen and purple curtains hung by cords of the finest linen and purple wool on silver rings, alabaster columns, gold and silver couches displayed on a surface made of valuable stones of alabaster, mother-of-pearl, and mineral stone. **1:7** Drinks were served in golden containers, all of which differed from one another. Royal wine was available in abundance at the king's expense. **1:8** There were no restrictions on the drinking, for the king had instructed all of his supervisors that they should do as everyone so desired. **1:9** Queen Vashti also gave a banquet for the women in King Ahasuerus' royal palace.

1:10 On the seventh day, as King Ahasuerus was feeling the effects of the wine, he ordered Mehuman, Biztha, Harbona, Bigtha, Abagtha, Zethar, and Carcas, the seven eunuchs who attended him, **1:11** to bring Queen Vashti into the king's presence wearing her royal high turban. He wanted to show the people and the officials her beauty, for she was very attractive. **1:12** But Queen Vashti refused to come at the king's bidding conveyed through the eunuchs. Then the king became extremely angry, and his rage consumed him.

1:13 The king then inquired of the wise men who were discerners of the times—for it was the royal custom to confer with all those who were proficient in laws and legalities. **1:14** Those who were closest to him were Carshena, Shethar, Admatha, Tarshish, Meres, Marsena, and Memucan. These men were the seven officials of Persia and Media who saw the king on a regular basis and had the most prominent offices in the kingdom. **1:15** The king asked, "By law, what should be done to Queen Vashti in light of the fact that she has not obeyed the instructions of King Ahasuerus conveyed through the eunuchs?"

1:16 Memucan then replied to the king and the officials, "The wrong of Queen Vashti is not against the king alone, but against all the officials and all the people who are throughout all the provinces of King Ahasuerus. **1:17** For the matter concerning the queen will spread to all the women, leading them to treat their husbands with contempt, saying, 'When King Ahasuerus gave orders to bring Queen Vashti into his presence, she would not come.' **1:18** And this very day the noble ladies of Persia and Media who have heard the matter concerning the queen will respond in the same way to all the royal officials, and there will be more than enough contempt and anger! **1:19** If the king is so inclined, let a royal edict go forth from him, and let it be written in the laws of Persia and Media that cannot be repealed, that Vashti may not come into the presence of King Ahasuerus, and let the king convey her royalty to another who is more deserving than she.

History tells us that Ahasuerus/ Xerxes probably embarked on his failed military campaigns in Europe, during which he was soundly defeated by the Greeks, between chapters one and two of Esther. You can read about the campaigns in Herodotus's The Histories, *particularly Book 7.*

1:20 And let the king's decision which he will enact be disseminated throughout all his kingdom, vast though it is. Then all the women will give honor to their husbands, from the most prominent to the lowly."

1:21 The matter seemed appropriate to the king and the officials. So the king acted on the advice of Memucan. **1:22** He sent letters throughout all the royal provinces, to each province according to its script and to each people according to its language, that every man should be ruling his family and should be speaking the language of his own people.

Esther 2

2:1 When these things had been accomplished and the rage of King Ahasuerus had diminished, he remembered Vashti and what she had done and what had been decided against her. **2:2** The king's servants who attended him said, "Let a search be conducted in the king's behalf for attractive young women. **2:3** And let the king appoint officers throughout all the provinces of his kingdom to gather all the attractive young women to Susa the citadel, to the harem under the authority of Hegai, the king's eunuch who oversees the women, and let him provide whatever cosmetics they desire. **2:4** Let the young woman whom the king finds most attractive become queen in place of Vashti." This seemed like a good idea to the king, so he acted accordingly.

2:5 Now there happened to be a Jewish man in Susa the citadel whose name was Mordecai. He was the son of Jair, the son of Shimei, the son of Kish, a Benjaminite, **2:6** who had been taken into exile from Jerusalem with the captives who had been carried into exile with Jeconiah king of Judah, whom Nebuchadnezzar king of Babylon had taken into exile. **2:7** Now he was acting as the guardian of Hadassah (that is, Esther), the daughter of his uncle, for neither her father nor her mother was alive. This young woman was very attractive and had a beautiful figure. When her father and mother died, Mordecai had raised her as if she were his own daughter.

2:8 It so happened that when the king's edict and his law became known many young women were taken to Susa the citadel to be placed under the authority of Hegai. Esther also was taken to the royal palace to be under the authority of Hegai, who was overseeing the women. **2:9** This young woman pleased him, and she found favor with him. He quickly provided her with her cosmetics and her rations; he also provided her with the seven special young women who were from the palace. He then transferred her and her young women to the best part of the harem.

2:10 Now Esther had not disclosed her people or her lineage, for Mordecai had instructed her not to do so. **2:11** And day after day Mordecai used to walk back and forth in front of the court of the harem in order to learn how Esther was doing and what might happen to her.

From history we can assume that King Ahasuerus is Xerxes I, who succeeded his father, Darius (485 BC). One of the historical sources that helps us identify Xerxes is the *Septuagint*. The term "Septuagint" is from the Latin word for "seventy" (abbreviated as LXX), which refers to the number of its translators. The LXX was a third century B.C. translation of the Hebrew scriptures into Greek. The LXX translators render Ahasuerus (Hebrew) as "Artaxerxes" (Greek). "Artaxerxes" was the Greek form of the name identified with several Persian kings, and though Xerxes I (or Ahasuerus) is called "Artaxerxes" in the Septuagint, he is not to be confused with Artaxerxes I, his successor, who reigned from 464–424 BC. The king in our story, Xerxes I, was known to have invaded Greece with a huge army. Yet only about five thousand returned. It was after his disastrous Greek campaign that Xerxes chose Esther as queen.

2. What do you learn about Ahasuerus from the following:

A. The extent of his kingdom (Esther 1:1)?

_____

_____

B. His economic status (Esther 1:4, 6, 7)?

_____

_____

C. His attitude about monogamy (Esther 2:4, 6–19)? Herodotus makes mention of Xerxes' illegitimate sons (*The Histories* 8.107).

_____

_____

D. His attitude about the genocide of his own subjects (Esther 3:8–11)?

_____

_____

E. Sometimes this story is told somewhat like *The King and I* as a great love story between a kind king and a holy girl. How does that portrayal compare to what you find in the biblical text?

_____

_____

_____

1. What do you know about Esther so far?
Her Hebrew name is:
A. Zeresh
B. Shushan
C. Purim
D. Hadassah

The name means:
A. Star
B. Myrtle
C. Thorn
D. Saturn

She was raised by her
A. Uncle
B. Cousin
C. Older brother
D. Adoptive parents

2. Esther was a Jewish woman living in a pagan land. Back when the Israelites were about to conquer the Promised Land, they received a command to refrain from intermarrying with its inhabitants, because they worshipped other gods (Deut. 7:1–4). Later, shortly after the time of Esther, the prophet Ezra expresses God's disfavor about those who have returned to their own land after serving as captives in Persian territory and intermarried with the people there.

A. What is Ezra's concern about intermarriage as seen in Ezra 9:1–2?

> **Ezra 9:1** Now when these things had been completed, the leaders approached me and said, "The people of Israel, the priests, and the Levites have not separated themselves from the local residents who practice detestable things similar to those of the Canaanites, the Hittites, the Perizzites, the Jebusites, the Ammonites, the Moabites, the Egyptians, and the Amorites. **9:2** Indeed, they have taken some of their daughters as wives for themselves and for their sons and have intermingled the holy seed with the local residents. Worse still, the leaders and the officials have been at the forefront of all of this!"

B. From what you know about how God felt about intermarriage with those who didn't worship Him and from what you know of King Xerxes, what does Esther's willingness to marry Xerxes suggest to you about her?

_____

_____

C. Read Leviticus 11:46–47.

> **Leviticus 11:46** This is the law of the land animals, the birds, all the living creatures that move in the water, and all the creatures that swarm on the land, **11:47** to distinguish between the unclean and the clean, between the living creatures that may be eaten and the living creatures that must not be eaten.

If no one in the palace has figured out that Esther is Jewish, what does that indicate about her observance of God's food laws?

_____

_____

3. Read Daniel 1:5, 8. How did Esther's actions during the "period of captivity" differ from those of Daniel?

> **Daniel 1:5** So the king assigned them a daily ration from his royal delicacies and from the wine he himself drank. They were to be trained for the next three years. At the end of that time they were to enter the king's service. **1:8** But Daniel made up his mind that he would not defile himself with the royal delicacies or the royal wine.

_____

_____

_____

_____

WEDNESDAY: MEET COUSIN MORDECAI

Note that we don't even meet the people who will be central to the outworking of God's plan in the story until the second chapter. God is at work before these key characters arrive on the scene.

1. What was Mordecai's nationality (Esther 2:5)?

_____

2. How did Mordecai end up in Susa when his people were from Judah (2:5–6)?

_____

_____

_____

_____

3. Aside from the fact that Mordecai was Esther's cousin, what other details do we know about his relationship to Esther (2:7, 11, 15)?

_____

_____

_____

4. What instructions had Mordecai given Esther about her nationality (2:10, 20)? Why do you suppose he might have done so?

_____

_____

_____

5. Where did Mordecai spend his time (2:19, 21)?

_____

_____

6. What was Mordecai's response to Haman (3:2–4)?

_____

_____

7. What was Mordecai's reason for refusing to pay homage to Haman (3:4)?

_____

_____

_____

THURSDAY: MEET HAMAN

1. The author is careful to give Haman a description that is significant in this story. What was his nationality (Esther 3:1)?

_____

2. Haman may have been a literal descendant of Agag, a well-known enemy of Israel. Yet after the slaughter of Agag's people, the term "Agagite" was also used metaphorically to identify those who were anti-Semitic.

> **15:7** Then Saul struck down the Amalekites all the way from Havilah to Shur, which is next to Egypt. **15:8** He captured King Agag of the Amalekites alive, but he executed all his people with the sword. **15:9** However, Saul and the army spared Agag, and the best of the flock, the cattle, the fatlings, and the lambs, as well as everything else that was of value. They were not willing to slaughter them. But they did slaughter everything that was despised and worthless.

3. In the Bible we meet Agag's ancestors after Moses led the people out of Egypt and are wandering in the wilderness. Read Exodus 17 (below).

> **Exodus 17:1** And all the community of the Israelites traveled on their journey from the Desert of Sin according to the instruction of the Lord, and they pitched camp in Rephidim. Now there was no water for the people to drink. **17:2** So the people strove with Moses, and they said, "Give us water to drink." Moses said to them, "Why do you strive with me? Why do you test the Lord?" **17:3** But the people thirsted there for water, and they murmured against Moses and said, "Why in the world did you bring us up out of Egypt—to kill us and our sons and our cattle with thirst?"
>
> **17:4** Then Moses cried out to the Lord, "What will I do with this people?—a little more and they will stone me!" **17:5** And the Lord said to Moses, "Go over before the people; take with you some of the elders of Israel and take in your hand your rod with which you struck the Nile and go. **17:6** I will be standing before you there on the rock in Horeb, and you will strike the rock, and water will come out of it so that the people may drink." And Moses did so in plain view of the elders of Israel.
>
> **17:7** And he called the name of the place Massah, and Meribah, because of the striving of the Israelites, and because of their testing the Lord, saying, "Is the Lord in our midst or not?"
>
> **17:8** Amalek came and attacked Israel in Rephidim. **17:9** So Moses said to Joshua, "Choose some of our men and go out, fight against Amalek. Tomorrow I will stand on top of the hill with the rod of God in my hand."
>
> **17:10** So Joshua fought against Amalek just as Moses had instructed him; and Moses and Aaron and Hur went up to the top of the hill. **17:11** And whenever Moses would raise his hands, then Israel prevailed; but whenever he would rest his hands, then Amalek prevailed. **17:12** When the hands of Moses became heavy, they took a stone and put it under him, and Aaron and Hur held up his hands, one on one side and one on the other, and so his hands were steady until the sun went down. **17:13** So Joshua destroyed Amalek and his army with the edge of the sword.

17:14 And the Lord said to Moses, "Write this as a memorial in the book, and rehearse it in Joshua's hearing; for I will surely wipe out the remembrance of Amalek from under the heavens. **17:15** And Moses built an altar; and he called it "The Lord is my Banner," **17:16** for he said, "For a hand was lifted up to the throne of the Lord—that the Lord will have war with Amalek from generation to generation."

4. According to what you have just read, who were the Amalekites and what had they done?

_____

_____

5. Read Deuteronomy 25:17–19. What was God's clear command about the Amalekites?

Deuteronomy 25:17 Remember what the Amalekites did to you on your way from Egypt, **25:18** how they met you along the way and cut off all your stragglers in the rear of the march when you were exhausted and tired; they were unafraid of God. **25:19** So when the Lord your God gives you relief from all the enemies who surround you in the land he is giving you as an inheritance, you must wipe the memory of the Amalekites from under heaven—do not forget!

_____

_____

_____

6. 1 Samuel 15 provides some information concerning the Amalekites that happened many years later.

15:1 Then Samuel said to Saul, "I was the one the Lord sent to anoint you as king over his people Israel. Now listen to what the Lord says. **15:2** Here is what the Lord of hosts says: 'I carefully observed how the Amalekites opposed Israel along the way when Israel came up from Egypt. **15:3** So go now and strike down the Amalekites. Destroy everything that they have. Don't spare them.

Put them to death—man, woman, child, infant, ox, sheep, camel, and donkey alike.'"

15:4 So Saul assembled the army and mustered them at Telaim. There were two hundred thousand foot soldiers and ten thousand men of Judah. **15:5** Saul proceeded to the city of Amalek, where he set an ambush in the wadi. **15:6** Saul said to the Kenites, "Go on and leave! Go down from among the Amalekites! Otherwise I will sweep you away with them! After all, you were kind to all the Israelites when they came up from Egypt." So the Kenites withdrew from among the Amalekites.

15:7 Then Saul struck down the Amalekites all the way from Havilah to Shur, which is next to Egypt. **15:8** He captured King Agag of the Amalekites alive, but he executed all his people with the sword. **15:9** However, Saul and the army spared Agag, and the best of the flock, the cattle, the fatlings, and the lambs, as well as everything else that was of value. They were not willing to slaughter them. But they did slaughter everything that was despised and worthless.

15:10 Then the word of the Lord came to Samuel, saying, **15:11** "I regret that I have made Saul king, for he has turned away from me and has not done what I said." Samuel became angry and he cried out to the Lord all that night.

15:12 Then Samuel got up early to meet Saul the next morning. But Samuel was informed, "Saul has gone to Carmel where he is setting up a monument for himself. Then Samuel left and went down to Gilgal." **15:13** When Samuel came to him, Saul said to him, "May the Lord bless you! I have done what the Lord said."

15:14 Samuel replied, "If that is the case, what then is this sound of sheep in my ears and the sound of cattle that I hear?" **15:15** Saul said, "They were brought from the Amalekites; the army spared the best of the flocks and cattle to sacrifice to the Lord our God. But everything else we slaughtered."

15:16 Then Samuel said to Saul, "Wait a minute! Let me tell you what the Lord said to me last night." He said to him, "Tell me." **15:17** Samuel said, "Is it not true that when you were insignificant in your own eyes, you became head of the tribes of Israel? The Lord chose you as king over Israel. **15:18** The Lord sent you on a campaign saying, 'Go and exterminate those sinful Amalekites! Fight against them until you have destroyed them.' **15:19** Why haven't you obeyed the Lord? Instead you have greedily rushed on the plunder. You have done what is wrong in the Lord's estimation."

15:20 Then Saul said to Samuel, "But I have obeyed the Lord! I went on the campaign the Lord sent me on. I brought back King Agag of the Amalekites, after exterminating the Amalekites. **15:21** But the army took from the plunder some of the sheep and cattle—the best of what was to be slaughtered—to sacrifice to the Lord your God in Gilgal."

15:22 Then Samuel said, "Does the Lord take pleasure in burnt offerings and sacrifices as much as he does in obedience? Certainly, obedience is better than sacrifice; paying attention is better than the fat of rams.

15:23 For rebellion is like the sin of divination, and presumption is like the evil of idolatry. Because you have rejected the word of the Lord, he has rejected you as king."

15:24 Then Saul said to Samuel, "I have sinned, for I have disobeyed what the Lord commanded and what you said as well. For I was afraid of the army, and I followed their wishes. **15:25** Now please forgive my sin. Go back with me so I can worship the Lord."

15:26 Samuel said to Saul, "I will not go back with you, for you have rejected the word of the Lord, and the Lord has rejected you from being king over Israel."

15:27 When Samuel turned to leave, Saul grabbed the edge of his robe and it tore. **15:28** Samuel said to him, "The Lord has torn the kingdom of Israel from you this day and has given it to one of your colleagues who is better than you! **15:29** The Preeminent One of Israel does not go back on his word or change his mind, for he is not a human being who changes his mind." **15:30** Saul again replied, "I have sinned. But please honor me before the elders of my people and before Israel. Go back with me so I may worship the Lord your God." **15:31** So Samuel followed Saul back, and Saul worshiped the Lord.

15:32 Then Samuel said, "Bring me King Agag of the Amalekites." So Agag came to him trembling, thinking to himself, "Surely death is bitter!" **15:33** Samuel said, "Just as your sword left women childless, so your mother will be the most bereaved among women." Then Samuel hacked Agag to pieces there in Gilgal before the Lord.

15:34 Then Samuel went to Ramah, while Saul went up to his home in Gibeah of Saul. **15:35** Until the day he died Samuel did not see Saul again. Samuel did, however, mourn for Saul, but the Lord regretted that he had made Saul king over Israel.

According to this chapter (printed below) what did God command King Saul to do with the Amalekites? And what did Saul actually do?

According to this chapter what did God command King Saul to do with the Amalekites? And what did Saul actually do?

_____

We read in verse 8 that Saul struck down all Agag's people with the sword. This could mean every single relative. Yet it could also mean only those engaged in battle—Agag's army. That would allow for the continuation of Agagite women and children, from whom Haman is descended. Many scholars believe Haman is a direct physical descendant of Agag.

7. Assuming Haman is a descendant of Agag, what did incomplete obedience to the command to wipe out the Amalekites cost Esther and her people?

_____

_____

_____

FRIDAY: MEET GOD

The Book of Esther does not mention God by name, or anything about religion or prayer. The closest we get is a reference to fasting. Yet a key message we take away after reading the entire book is that God is sovereign and He is faithful to show merciful, loyal love to His covenant people. What we learn about God's control of events is **covert** in Esther, but it's **overt** in other scriptures.

1. Read Psalm 11.

> **Psalm 11:1** In the Lord I have taken shelter. How can you say to me, "Flee to a mountain like a bird!
>
> **11:2** For look, the wicked prepare their bows, they put their arrows on the strings, to shoot in the darkness at the morally upright.
>
> **11:3** When the foundations are destroyed, what can the godly accomplish?"
>
> **11:4** The Lord is in his holy temple; the Lord's throne is in heaven. His eyes watch; his eyes examine all people.

11:5 The Lord approves of the godly, but he hates the wicked and those who love to do violence

11:6 May the Lord rain down burning coals and brimstone on the wicked! A whirlwind is what they deserve!

11:7 Certainly the Lord is just; he rewards godly deeds; the upright will experience his favor.

2. What does this psalm teach about God?

_____

_____

_____

3. Consider Psalm 11:4. His eyes watch and examine us. Spend time asking His help to make you righteous and godly. Confess known sin. Is there someone from whom you need to ask forgiveness?

_____

_____

_____

4. List events that are causing you pain—from family difficulties to the plight of Christians overseas facing martyrdom for their faith. Pray about them, acknowledging your trust of God's sovereignty in the midst of pain.

_____

_____

_____

SATURDAY: PRIDE AND PREJUDICE

This afternoon when I went to warm my lunch, I wondered if my microwave had a malfunction because it took longer than two minutes for my soup to heat up. It wasn't broken; the problem was my impatience.

Most of us are not so good at waiting well.

But God isn't like us. He's extremely patient, especially when it comes to meting out justice. Take for example how he evens the score with the Baal-worshiping Queen Jezebel.

Jezebel's husband, King Ahab of Israel, sees a vineyard he wants over in Jezreel. But the vineyard owner doesn't want to sell it to Ahab or exchange it for another (we find the story in 1 Kings 21). So King Ahab pouts; in fact, he's so sullen he refuses to eat. Well, when Jezebel hears about it, she bribes some officials to give such awful false witness against the vineyard owner that he ends up getting stoned to death. Then Ahab doesn't even have to pay for the vineyard. It's all his.

Just one problem: this action by Ahab and Jezebel makes God very angry. And God swears He will avenge the injustice. But then He waits. And waits.

And a few years go by.

How can He be so patient?

More years go by.

But then (fast forward to 2 Kings 9) some of Jezebel's servants throw her out the window and when they go to bury her, they find only her skull, feet, and the palms of her hands. Dogs have eaten her. And you want to know where her body lies? In Jezreel—the very place where she instigated the injustice. Poetic, isn't it? (if gore can be poetic).

God was and is also patient with His own people. He had given them some clear instructions about destroying all the Amalekites, a nation that loathed the Israelites and posed a serious threat to them. But the Israelites kept falling short of complete obedience.

The Book of Esther gives us an example of the consequences. Mordecai, a Jew, refuses to bow to Haman, an Amalekite. So Haman seethes over it. Rabbinic tradition holds that Haman was the descendant of an Amalekite king, and as such, he is is willing to pay big money to wipe out his enemies. He goes so far as to offer King Xerxes ten thousand talents of silver to destroy the Jews (3:9).

Now, how much exactly is that? Would it be like a millionaire offering ten thousand dollars?

No, it's more. Way more. According to Herodotus's *The Histories*,[3] the annual revenue of the entire Persian Empire was 14,560

---

[3] *Histories* 3:95.<www.iranchamber.com/history/herodotus/herodotus_history_book3.php>

Euboean talents. After you adjust for the kind of money used, you find that Haman's offer comes to the equivalent of about two-thirds of the royal income. And he probably intended to pay this enormous sum from the profits gained by plundering property (3:13).

Keep in mind the times. The king has just spent a few years losing close to two million soldiers in a failed campaign against the Greeks, so his personal wealth used to finance the wars has probably been depleted. The king replies to Haman's offer with, "The silver is given to you." Now, most have understood this to mean that the king turned down the money. But one translator reads it as the king accepting the offer, giving the same sort of response we offer when we see someone blowing a wad of cash: "Hey, it's your money!" (That is, "I think you're crazy, but waste it if you like.") The fact that Mordecai knows the amount (4:7) and Esther says later "I and my people have been sold" (7:4) indicate there may be some validity to this latter interpretation.

Whether or not the king profited financially, the bottom line is this: Haman's outrageous offer is fueled by nothing more than pride and prejudice.

All of this terror for Esther and her people could have been avoided if only the children of Israel had listened to the Lord and obeyed Him long ago. If only they had followed His commands.... But perhaps they reasoned that the Lord's decrees were too harsh.

If only....

What commands has God given us that we're failing to fully obey? To pray without ceasing? To give thanks in all things? To treat our bodies as temples worthy of His Spirit's presence? To wait on Him? To deny ourselves?

Often we may ask God's will for our lives. We may inquire about what job to take, whom to marry, where to go to school. But He is much more concerned about who we are on the job, how we act in our singleness or with our spouses, what kind of character we have in the classroom.

He is patient. But He also demands our complete obedience both for His glory and our good. Spare yourself—and future generations—the pain. Decide today that with His help you won't disobey or delay for another minute.

Prayer: *Heavenly Father, thank You for Your Word and how You use it to reveal Yourself and Your plans to and for me. Thank You for Your infinite patience with Your people, including me. Forgive my willingness* *to put my own interests ahead of Yours. Show me those areas of my life where I'm failing to apply what I already know and grant me the grace to love and obey You wholeheartedly. In the name of Your Son, Amen.*

For Memorization: "The Lord is not slow about His promise, as some count slowness, but is patient toward you, not wishing for any to perish but for all to come to repentance." (2 Peter 3:9 NASB)

WEEK 3 OF 5

The Ecstasy and the Agony: Esther 2:11—4:9

SUNDAY: HE THINKS HE'S ALL THAT

Scripture: *When Haman saw that Mordecai neither bowed down nor paid homage to him, Haman was filled with rage. But he disdained to lay hands on Mordecai alone, for they had told him who the people of Mordecai were; therefore Haman sought to destroy all the Jews, the people of Mordecai, who were throughout the whole kingdom of Ahasuerus.* (Esther 3:5–6)

In recognition of my birthday this year, two friends took me to Starbucks for some girl time. As we sat sipping tall lattes, we bemoaned the fact that we no longer comprehend the language of youth. "We're getting old" we groaned. And that would be fine, we reasoned, in countries such as China or Russia where people respect age. But not in North America.

Having mastered early twenty-first century idioms such as "the blogosphere," we had grown sadly complacent, thinking we were hip beyond our years. But then we learned that "Benjamins" and "dead presidents" were references to money—not *new* references to money, mind you. But references that lots of people already know and have known for a long time. Who knew?

Apparently 'most everybody but us.

It reminded me of a time several years earlier when my daughter, in trying to explain the sorry attitude of one of her classmates, exhaled and summed it up with a phrase: "She thinks she's all that."

Come again? Revealing myself to be a total flatliner (the new term for "braindead"), I answered with, "I thought 'She's All That' was a movie title."

And there it was—that exhale again—along with the "duh" look. "Mo-o-m, the movie is *about* a girl who's all that."

"Oh. Of course."

My daughter went on to explain that "all that" means superior.

Some months later I was reading the Book of Esther, and I thought of my daughter's explanation when I read about Haman. The description fits: He thinks he's all that—and more! The first time he gets hacked off at Mordecai it's because "Cousin Mordy" refuses to bow or pay homage (3:2, 5). Haman is further enraged when Mordecai refuses to stand up and tremble (5:9). The Persians took that bowing stuff seriously. It wasn't like our custom of bowing to royalty today. Nobody mistakes that common courtesy for worship. But Persian bowing was often associated with emperor or magistrate worship. So although Haman's income is equivalent to the GNP of several developing countries, here he is fussing that some little nobody, some mere gnat (from his perspective) refused to treat him like a god?

And boy, is he worried. This worry drives Haman to thoughts of unspeakable violence. He plots genocide against Mordecai's people (3:6), offers the king ten thousand silver talents to be rid of them (3:9), and has a gallows (literally in Hebrew: "tree") built especially for spiking Mordecai's body after his death (5:14). Does Haman have an ego problem or what?

Haman is a great example demonstrating "God is opposed to the proud, but gives grace to the humble." Haman intends honor for himself, but he ends up having to honor Mordecai. Though he builds gallows for Mordecai, he ends up getting himself spiked along with his sons. Haman seeks to destroy all of God's people, but in the end none of God's people die; however, Haman's family faces extermination.

Think about company slogans that tell us we're center-orbit. "You deserve a break today"; "We're not number one—you are"; "Have it your way!"; "Obey your thirst!" or "Just do it." Our culture encourages our me-focused thinking, though we don't need much help.

Still, hopefully we know there's a reason the planet is called "Earth" and not Sanworld, Maryworld, Alisonworld, (your name) world.

Pride has many forms. Sometimes it shows up as false humility. It can also be in-your-face arrogance. Consider the engineer who said of the *Titanic* that God Himself couldn't sink it. Or the Beatle who said "We're more popular than Jesus." Or Nietzsche, who insisted, "God is dead." Where are their voices now?

Pride can look like the Pharisees, who publicly thanked God they were not sinners of the bigtime variety. It can also take the form of racism. Haman's hatred is certainly racially motivated.

Do you want to receive God's grace? Do you want to avoid His opposing you? "God is opposed to the proud" but the flip side of that is that "He gives grace to the humble" (James 4:6; 1 Pet. 5:5). So humble yourself. There's only One who's all that—*the Lord Himself.*

MONDAY: THE UNSEEN HAND AT WORK

1. Pray asking God for insight and then read Esther 2:11—4:11.

> **Esther 2:11** And day after day Mordecai used to walk back and forth in front of the court of the harem in order to learn how Esther was doing and what might happen to her.
>
> **2:12** At the end of the twelve months that were required for the women, when the turn of each young woman arrived to go to King Ahasuerus—for in this way they had to fulfill their time of cosmetic treatment: six months in oil of myrrh, and six months in perfume and various ointments used by women—**2:13** the woman would go to the king in the following way: Whatever she asked for would be provided for her to take with her from the harem to the royal palace. **2:14** In the evening she went, and in the morning she returned to a separate part of the harem, to the authority of Shaashgaz the king's eunuch who was overseeing the concubines. She would not go back to the king unless the king was pleased with her and she was requested by name.
>
> **2:15** When it became the turn of Esther daughter of Abihail the uncle of Mordecai (who had raised her as if she were his own daughter) to go to the king, she did not request any thing except

for what Hegai the king's eunuch, who was overseer of the women, had recommended. Yet Esther met with the approval of all who saw her. **2:16** Then Esther was taken to King Ahasuerus at his royal residence in the tenth month (that is, the month of Tebeth) in the seventh year of his reign. **2:17** And the king loved Esther more than all the other women, and she met with his loving approval more than all the other young women. So he placed the royal high turban on her head and appointed her queen in place of Vashti. **2:18** Then the king prepared a large banquet for all his officials and his servants—it was actually Esther's banquet. He also set aside a holiday for the provinces, and he provided for offerings at the king's expense.

2:19 Now when the young women were being gathered again, Mordecai was sitting at the king's gate. **2:20** Esther was still not divulging her lineage or her people, just as Mordecai had instructed her. Esther continued to do whatever Mordecai said, just as she had done when he was raising her.

2:21 In those days while Mordecai was sitting at the king's gate, Bigthan and Teresh, two of the king's eunuchs who protected the entrance, got angry and plotted to assassinate King Ahasuerus. **2:22** When Mordecai learned of the conspiracy, he informed Queen Esther, and Esther told the king in Mordecai's behalf. **2:23** The king then had the matter investigated and, finding it to be so, had the two conspirators hanged on a gallows. It was then recorded in the daily chronicles in the king's presence.

Esther 3

3:1 Sometime later King Ahasuerus promoted Haman the son of Hammedatha, the Agagite, exalting him and setting his position above that of all the officials who were with him. **3:2** As a result, all the king's servants who were at the king's gate were bowing and paying homage to Haman, for the king had so commanded. However, Mordecai did not bow, nor did he pay him homage.

3:3 Then the servants of the king who were at the king's gate asked Mordecai, "Why are you violating the king's commandment?" **3:4** And after they had spoken to him day after day without his paying any attention to them, they informed Haman to see whether this attitude on Mordecai's part would be permitted. Furthermore, he had disclosed to them that he was a Jew.

3:5 When Haman saw that Mordecai was not bowing or paying homage to him, he was filled with rage. **3:6** But the thought of striking out against Mordecai alone was repugnant to him, for he had been informed of the identity of Mordecai's people. So Haman sought to destroy all the Jews (that is, the people of Mordecai) who were in all the kingdom of Ahasuerus.

3:7 In the first month (that is, the month of Nisan), in the twelfth year of King Ahasuerus' reign, *pur* (that is, the lot) was cast before Haman in order to determine a day and a month. It turned out to be the twelfth month (that is, the month of Adar).

3:8 Then Haman said to King Ahasuerus, "There is a particular people that is dispersed and spread throughout the inhabitants in all the provinces of your kingdom whose laws differ from those of all other peoples. Furthermore, they do not observe the king's laws. It is not appropriate for the king to provide a haven for them. **3:9** If the king is so inclined, let an edict be issued to destroy them. I will pay ten thousand talents of silver to be conveyed to the king's treasuries for the officials who carry out this business."

3:10 So the king removed his signet ring from his hand and gave it to Haman the son of Hammedatha, the Agagite, who was hostile toward the Jews. **3:11** The king replied to Haman, "Keep your money, and do with those people whatever you wish."

3:12 So the royal scribes were summoned in the first month, on the thirteenth day of the month. Everything Haman commanded was written to the king's satraps and governors who were in every province and to the officials of every people, province by province according to its script and people by people according to its language. In the name of King Ahasuerus it was written and sealed with the king's signet ring. **3:13** Letters were sent by the runners to all the king's provinces stating that they should destroy, kill, and annihilate all the Jews, from youth to elderly, both women and children, on a particular day, namely the thirteenth day of the twelfth month (that is, the month of Adar), and to loot and plunder their possessions. **3:14** A copy of this edict was to be presented as law throughout every province; it was to be made known to all the inhabitants, so that they would be prepared for this day. **3:15** The messengers scurried forth with the king's order. The edict was issued in Susa the citadel. While the king and Haman sat down to drink, the city of Susa was in an uproar!

Esther 4

4:1 Now when Mordecai became aware of all that had been done, he tore his garments and put on sackcloth and ashes. He went out into the city, crying out in a loud and bitter voice. **4:2** But he went no further than the king's gate, for no one was permitted to enter the king's gate clothed in sackcloth. **4:3** Throughout each and every province where the king's edict and law were announced there was considerable mourning among the Jews, along with fasting, weeping, and sorrow. Sackcloth and ashes were characteristic of many. **4:4** When Esther's female attendants and her eunuchs came and informed her about Mordecai's behavior, the queen was overcome with anguish. Although she sent garments for Mordecai to put on so that he could remove his sackcloth, he would not accept them. **4:5** So Esther called for Hathach, one of the king's eunuchs who had been placed at her service, and instructed him to find out the cause and reason for Mordecai's behavior. **4:6** So Hathach went to Mordecai at the plaza of the city in front of the king's gate. **4:7** Then Mordecai related to him everything that had happened to him, even the specific amount of money that Haman had offered to pay to the king's treasuries for the Jews to be destroyed. **4:8** He also gave him a written copy of the law that had been disseminated in Susa for their destruction so that he could show it to Esther and talk to her about it. He also gave instructions that she should go to the king to implore him and petition him in behalf of her people. **4:9** So Hathach returned and related Mordecai's instructions to Esther.

2. Summarize what you have just read. What happens?

_____

_____

3. How do you think Esther and Mordecai felt when they had learned Esther was the king's favorite?

_____

_____

4. How do you think Mordecai felt when he learned of the evil edict (see 4:1)?

_____

_____

5. Have you ever gone from a high place to a low place? What happened? How did it feel?

_____

_____

TUESDAY: THE CHOICE

1. Read Esther 2:11–14. Sometimes what remains unsaid speaks volumes. Do you think the king sat and looked at Esther, found her pretty, and that's all that happened during "her night with the king"? Why or why not?

_____

_____

_____

2. What are some indications that God is at work in and through Esther, even though Esther is not necessarily following His law?

_____

_____

_____

3. Read Esther 2:19. What does the gathering of virgins (young women) a second time indicate about the king's ongoing satisfaction with Esther alone?

_____

_____

_____

4. God later uses the very position Esther has gained (possibly through questionable means) to accomplish the salvation of His people. In doing so He demonstrates that He can use even our sins for His glory. If you walk into a pregnancy resource center today and talk to the staff, you'll find that in many cases some of these staff members had abortions in the past and they're using what they've learned from their mistakes to minister to those faced with similar choices. Take a few moments to offer to God any regrettable decisions you've made, asking Him to use them for His purposes. Do you need to take it a step further? (Make a call, volunteer, write a letter?)

_____

_____

_____

WEDNESDAY: GOOD NEWS, BAD NEWS

1. The assassination plot is revealed. What does Mordecai do as recorded in 2:21–23? And what risks does he take in doing so?

_____

_____

_____

_____

> It might be easy to applaud Mordecai's refusal to bow as an indication of his spiritual faithfulness in identifying with God's people. Yet it's equally possible that his behavior stems from his nationalism rather than from his desire to honor God.

2. Why does Mordecai refuse to bow to Haman (3:4)? What risks does he take in doing so?

_____

_____

_____

3. How does Haman react to Mordecai's behavior (see 3:6, 9 and 5:14)?

_____

_____

_____

_____

4. What might be your response if your government declared a day in which everyone who killed God's people would get large sums of money?

_____

_____

_____

_____

5. What was the response to the edict on the part of Mordecai and the Jewish people (4:1–3)?

_____

_____

_____

_____

THURSDAY: DARKNESS BEFORE DAWN

1. Read Esther 3:7. Haman cast the lot. On New Year's Day in the Ancient Near East, people often made all their plans for the year using "astrological guidance." Haman cast *pur* or lots to determine the best date for the annihilation of God's people, and the lot determined that

twelve months would pass before the event. Who was Haman's real "astrological guide?" What irony do you see in his consulting the stars for the date?

_____

_____

_____

_____

2. What was Haman's accusation against Mordecai's people (3:8)? Do you think he was telling the truth? What half-truths does he appear to tell?

> *The imprint of the king's ring was the equivalent of his signature in ancient times. In a world without TV images or photos, people could pass themselves off as being more important than they were. Who would know? The people might not know what their monarch looked like. But a signet ring bore the king's seal, which was a way of identifying something as being from the king. (See Esther 3:10.)*

_____

_____

_____

3. What was the gist of Haman's edict (3:13)?

_____

_____

4. List circumstances in your world today that seem outside of God's control. Spend some time asking Him to work behind the scenes personally, nationally, globally.

_____

_____

_____

5. Note circumstances in your life right now or in the lives of those you love in which it sometimes feels as though God is absent. Then spend some time asking for Him to be glorified through the difficulties and to make His presence known.

FRIDAY: SOMETIMES IT LOOKS LIKE ALL IS LOST

1. Reread Esther 4:1–9. Note again Mordecai's response to the edict (4:1).

---

2. Keep in mind that Mordecai could not have ongoing contact with Esther once she was made queen. (There was a reason a king typically had eunuchs attending his queen—he had to be sure any heirs were of actual royal lineage. So most queens had only limited contact with men.) When and how did Esther finally learn about Haman's plot?

---

3. According to 4:8, what does Mordecai think Esther should do?

---

4. It's easy to read this story a few thousand years later, knowing how it will end, and feel no threat. Most marriages we know of are, at least to some degree, partnerships. But Esther's husband is not her soul companion. They don't share their lives together, and she could die for annoying him. Use your imagination and consider what such a marriage might be like:

_____

_____

_____

_____

5. Are you facing situations in which you, like Esther and with God's help, need to show courage? One of the messages of the Book of Esther is that God is in control. Talk to the sovereign, almighty Father about what's on your heart.

_____

_____

_____

_____

6. Spend some time thanking God for the unseen work He does in your life, church, and world, from specific protections to the world-wide outworking of events. Praise Him that His ultimate plans are never thwarted. Write a short, concluding prayer below.

_____

_____

_____

_____

SATURDAY: PUTTING IT IN REVERSE

Our God is a God of great reversals, especially where His people and His promises are concerned. The Book of Esther is full of such reversals. A queen is deposed; an orphaned young woman takes her place. A man who starts out hiding his nationality is exalted as his people's spokesperson. A nation bound for destruction triumphs over its enemies.

Millennia before the Book of Esther, God had promised to make of Abraham a great nation and guaranteed that through him all the nations of the earth would be blessed. God kept that promise through Esther in preserving Abraham's descendents from destruction.

What has God promised *you*? A great nation? Well, no. Deliverance from every difficulty? Certainly not, though in His mercy God often spares us. Take for example the children in the World Vision orphanage, who "happened" to be gone on an outing when the 2004 tsunami in East Asia destroyed their entire community. Mercy!

But God does not always spare us from tragedy. In Banda Aceh, Indonesia, a small group of believers lost seventeen in that same tsunami.

God's sparing us of all tragedy wouldn't square with Jesus' pronouncement to the disciples that "in the world you will have tribulation" (John 16:33) or with Paul's exhortation to Timothy to endure hardship (2 Tim. 4:5).

What, then, has God promised members of Christ's body, the church? Among other things, He is always with us (Heb. 13:5). And He works all things together for good (Rom. 8:28). Really? *All* things? Even terrorist attacks? And tsunamis? What about divorce? And rebellious children? And alcoholism? What about all our deep unfulfilled longings? *All* things?

All things.

Our Lord is the author of great reversals. Esther's story doesn't end with Mordecai facing the gallows. And hundreds of years after that, Jesus' story doesn't end with an earthquake on Good Friday.

Make a mental list of the difficulties you and your loved ones are facing today. They hurt, don't they?

God promises that He's with you. Even if you can't see or feel Him, the Lord is near, and He cares. He can give you the supernatural strength to endure, to trust, to obey, even (perhaps especially) if your heart is broken or you're weary and worn down. Talk to Him.

God promises to work all your difficulties together for good. That doesn't mean the trials themselves are good—only that God can work them together for good. Nothing in our lives happens to us without first passing through the loving hands of our Father, so there's nothing we face that He cannot use or that takes Him by surprise. Even Esther's compromises didn't thwart His purposes.

Ask God to do a grand reversal in your life. Ask Him to turn your sin into yet another way to magnify His glorious name. Give Him your broken pieces and ask Him to make something good of them.

Prayer: *Heavenly Father, thank You that You are the God of reversals. Thank You that You can use even my sins to ultimately bring glory to Yourself. Make me holy, cleansed, and available for Your service. What would You have me be? What would You have me do? Thank You for the peace that passes understanding. Help me to show others the kind of unmerited favor and forgiveness You have extended to me. In the name of Your perfect Son, Amen.*

For Memorization: "Their trouble was turned to happiness and their mourning to a holiday. These were to be days of banqueting, happiness, sending gifts to one another, and providing for the poor." (Esth. 9:22)

WEEK 4 OF 5

The Reluctant Heroine: Esther 4:10—5:14

SUNDAY: THE SECOND-CHANCE GOD

Scripture: *"For if you remain silent at this time, relief and deliverance will arise for the Jews from another place and you and your father's house will perish. And who knows whether you have not attained royalty for such a time as this?"* (Esther 4:14 NASB)

We often think of Esther as a heroine. After all because of her actions, an entire people group was spared their own genocide.

Yet what is heroism, really? It's opportunity plus courage. Think of the daily work of firefighters and police officers. Heroism is often seen in an ordinary person showing courage in an extraordinary circumstance. Fear, though there, is cast aside as one places others' welfare above one's own. Sometimes, as in Esther's case, the valiant choice doesn't get made on the first try. Esther ultimately made the best decision. But consider this rough paraphrase of her initial response to Mordecai's bad news: "Uh, you expect me to go talk to the king? Are you kidding? I could *die* for 'outing' myself. It's not like the king and I hang out a lot. Do you recall what he did to the last wife who displeased him? It's been a month since he even wanted to be with me."

I'm not trying to minimize the heroism of the choice Esther finally made. She risked her very life. But here's my point: she was just an ordinary girl with a really big God.

Just like us.

Notice the answer Mordecai sends back to her. Is it full of father-like empathy? No! His answer goes something like this: "What makes you think you'll survive by hiding while the rest of us die? If you keep quiet, you and your relatives *will* die, even when someone else comes along and liberates us all." So is Mordecai threatening to "out" her if she doesn't out herself? Many scholars think so. Whether or not he is, he doesn't leave it there. He ends positively by suggesting there's a design behind all the events that have led to her living in the palace. Mordecai's closing words, which hint at the sovereignty of God, are the theme verse for the entire book: "It may very well be that you have achieved royal status for such a time as this!"

We often think of heroism as something done on a grand scale— of deeds such as Churchill's urging the British Empire on to her "finest hour." Yet God's kind of heroism takes many forms. It might indeed have far-reaching consequences such as the actions of Esther. Or of Rosa Parks during the civil rights movement, refusing to sit in the back of the bus. Or Mother Teresa caring for the destitute in Calcutta. Yet others' heroism may have no audience. Consider the courage of the following individuals.

- Mary, with small children, longed to be in the marketplace hearing complete sentences, but she chose to stay home with her kids attacking mounds of laundry during those crucial developmental years.
- Nancy, who had breast cancer, found the courage to hold her hairless head high sporting brilliantly colored turbans. In the process she lifted the spirits of all around her.
- Sanshay gave away the only coat he had because someone else needed it more.
- Kerri never dreamed God would ever call any mom to enroll her child in pre-school. Yet she sensed He was doing that very thing with her so she could attend language school in preparation for ministry with her husband. The result? "It was the hardest thing I've ever done, but my daughter has thrived."

- Fran changed her mother's bed pan several times a day for ten years.
- Jim gave up his Christmas break to lead a team to work with the poor.

Sometimes in American Christendom we get enamored with high-profile leaders. And then we're tempted to think all truly spiritual people are famous, while the lesser mortals are somehow lacking in spiritual vitality. Yet God has no such scale for measuring worth. There's a reward even for the minute act of giving a cup of water (Matt. 10:42). It doesn't have to be a skyscraper dedication to get His attention. Nor the donation of a hospital wing. Just a drink.

One of our family's favorite seminary professors is known to sometimes say, "Decrease your vision." While some of us do need to step into the broad arena and do big things for God, most of us, instead of running off to "save the world," need to be heroes for smaller audiences, even if those audiences this side of heaven consist only of the angels who see our good works done in secret.

What "opportunities" are facing you? Maybe you've lacked courage and already said "no" to God's initial prompting. Esther did. But that's not the end of her story. What about yours?

MONDAY: FOR SUCH A TIME AS THIS

1. Pray asking the Lord to give you insight. Then read Esther 4:10—5:14.

> **Esther 4:10** Then Esther replied to Hathach with instructions for Mordecai: **4:11** "All the servants of the king and the people of the king's provinces know that there is only one law applicable to any man or woman who comes uninvited to the king in the inner court—that person will be put to death, unless the king extends to him the gold scepter, permitting him to be spared. Now I have not been invited to come to the king for some thirty days!"
>
> **4:12** When Esther's reply was conveyed to Mordecai, **4:13** he said to take back this answer to Esther: **4:14** "Don't imagine that because you are part of the king's household you will be the one Jew who will escape. If you keep quiet at this time, liberation and protection for the Jews will appear from another source, while you and your father's household perish. It may very well be that you

have achieved royal status for such a time as this!"

4:15 Then Esther sent this reply to Mordecai: **4:16** "Go, assemble all the Jews who are found in Susa and fast in my behalf. Don't eat and don't drink for three days, night or day. My female attendants and I will also fast in the same way. Afterward I will go to the king, even though it violates the law. If I perish, I perish!"

4:17 So Mordecai set out to do everything that Esther had instructed him.

Esther 5

5:1 It so happened that on the third day Esther put on her royal attire and stood in the inner court of the palace, opposite the king's quarters. The king was sitting on his royal throne in the palace, opposite the entrance. **5:2** When the king saw Queen Esther standing in the court, she met with his approval. The king extended to Esther the gold scepter that was in his hand, and Esther approached and touched the end of the scepter.

5:3 The king said to her, "What is on your mind, Queen Esther? What is your request? Even as much as half the kingdom will be given to you!"

5:4 Esther replied, "If the king is so inclined, let the king and Haman come today to the banquet that I have prepared for him." **5:5** The king replied, "Find Haman quickly so that we can do as Esther requests."

So the king and Haman went to the banquet that Esther had prepared. **5:6** While at the banquet of wine, the king said to Esther, "What is your request? It shall be given to you. What is your petition? Ask for as much as half the kingdom, and it shall be done!"

5:7 Esther responded, "My request and my petition is this: **5:8** If I have found favor in the king's sight and if the king is inclined to grant my request and perform my petition, let the king and Haman come tomorrow to the banquet that I will prepare for them. At that time I will do as the king wishes.

5:9 Now Haman went forth that day pleased and very much encouraged. But when Haman saw Mordecai at the king's gate, and he did not rise nor tremble in his presence, Haman was filled with rage toward Mordecai. **5:10** But Haman restrained himself and went on to his home.

He then sent for his friends to join him, along with his wife Zeresh. **5:11** Haman then recounted to them his fabulous wealth, his many sons, and how the king had magnified him and exalted him over the king's other officials and servants. **5:12** Haman said, "Furthermore, Esther the queen invited only me to accompany the king to the banquet that she prepared! And also tomorrow I am invited along with the king. **5:13** Yet all of this fails to satisfy me so long as I have to see Mordecai the Jew sitting at the king's gate."

5:14 Haman's wife Zeresh and all his friends said to him, "Have a gallows seventy-five feet high built, and in the morning tell the king that Mordecai should be hanged on it. Then go satisfied with the king to the banquet."

It seemed like a good idea to Haman, so he had the gallows built.

2. What stands out to you in this section?

_____

_____

_____

TUESDAY: THE FEAR

1. What was Esther's initial response to the news about Haman's plot (4:11)?

_____

_____

_____

2. What was Esther's second response, given after Mordecai challenged her (4:16)?

_____

_____

_____

3. What did she see as her fate, either way?

_____

_____

4. Shortly after Esther was made queen, the virgins were gathered together again for the king (see 2:19). At the time she heard of Haman's plot, the king had not summoned Esther for a month (4:11). What might we surmise from this about how much clout Esther had with him?

_____

_____

_____

5. Read 4:16. What do you think Esther was feeling?

_____

_____

Herodotus, who lived in the fifth century B.C., is commonly called the "father of history." You can pick up his work, The Histories, *for under ten dollars in paperback. His way of recording history is not what we generally consider "historical" or completely reliable factually, but he does provide some interesting information. He covers events ranging from the pharaohs in 3000 BC to the defeat of the Persians in the fifth century BC. He provides some information about Persian rule that's of particular interest to those studying Esther: "Deioces introduced for the first time the ceremonial of royalty: admission to the king's presence was forbidden, and all communication had to be through messengers."[4]*

[4] Herodotus, *The Histories,* 1.99. Deioces was the first of the Median kings. The bust in the photo above resides at the National Museum of Naples.

6. Think back to a situation in the past (or one you're currently facing) in which doing the right thing meant taking risks. What happened? What was your initial response?

_____

_____

_____

_____

WEDNESDAY: THE PURIM DIET

1. Read 4:16. What do you think Esther has in mind when she asks everyone to fast? (Hint: It's not weight loss.)

_____

_____

_____

2. Have you ever fasted? If so, for how long? Did you drink anything during the time you were fasting?

_____

_____

_____

_____

3. Describe the kind of fast Esther has in mind. How long does it last? Of what does it consist?

_____

_____

_____

4. While Esther is fasting, what is she doing (5:4)? What do you think would be challenging about that?

_____

_____

_____

_____

5. As we've seen, the Book of Esther does not refer overtly to God. Yet why do you think Esther tells everyone to fast?

_____

_____

_____

> How long can someone survive without water? Healthy people can last about a week. But they might want to die after about the second day. Some fasts are water-only. Others are juice-only. Some last from sunup to sundown, with feasting after dark. Most today who observe the annual fast of Esther do so with a one-day, daytime-only fast. Some fast an additional three days; others include the night as well as the day. But a three–day, round-the-clock, no-food-or-drink fast such as Esther proposes suggests a truly desperate situation.

A. Read the words below spoken by King David after his son dies. What does he imply about his view of the purpose of fasting?

2 Samuel 12:23 But now he is dead. Why should I fast? Am I able to bring him back? I will go to him, but he cannot return to me!

_____

_____

B. What was the purpose of Jehoshaphat's fast?

> **2 Chr. 20:3–4** Jehoshaphat was afraid, so he decided to seek the Lord's advice. He decreed that all Judah should observe a fast. **20:4** The people of Judah assembled to ask for the Lord's help; they came from all the cities of Judah to ask for the Lord's help.

_____

_____

_____

C. What activities were associated with the psalmist's fast?

> **Psalm 69:9–13**
>
> Certainly devotion to your temple consumes me; I endure the insults of those who insult you.
>
> I weep and refrain from eating food, which causes others to insult me.
>
> I wear sackcloth and they ridicule me.
>
> Those who sit at the city gate talk about me; drunkards mock me in their songs.
>
> O Lord, may you hear my prayer and be favorably disposed to me!

_____

_____

_____

D. What are God's purposes in the fast described in Isaiah?

> **Isaiah 58:4–10** Look, your fasting is accompanied by arguments, brawls, and fist fights. Do not fast as you do today, trying to make your voice heard in heaven. Is this really the kind of fasting I want? Do I want a day when people just humble themselves, bowing their heads like a reed and stretching out on sackcloth and ashes? Is this really what you call a fast, a day that is pleasing to the

Lord? No, this is the kind of fast I want. I want you to remove the sinful chains, to tear away the ropes of the burdensome yoke, to set free the oppressed, and to break every burdensome yoke. I want you to share your food with the hungry and to provide shelter for homeless, oppressed people. When you see someone naked, clothe him! Don't turn your back on your own flesh and blood! Then your light will shine like the sunrise; your restoration will quickly arrive; your godly behavior will go before you, and the Lord's splendor will be your rear guard. Then you will call out, and the Lord will respond; you will cry out, and he will reply, 'Here I am.' You must remove the burdensome yoke from among you and stop pointing fingers and speaking sinfully. You must actively help the hungry and feed the oppressed. Then your light will dispel the darkness, and your darkness will be transformed into noonday.

_____

_____

_____

E. Does Jesus expect that His disciples will fast (Matthew 6:16–18)? What does He have to say about fasting?

> **Matthew 6:16–18** "When you fast, do not look sullen like the hypocrites, for they make their faces unattractive so that people will see them fasting. I tell you the truth, they have their reward. When you fast, put oil on your head and wash your face, so that it will not be obvious to others when you are fasting, but only to your Father who is in secret. And your Father, who sees in secret, will reward you.

_____

_____

_____

F. Do you fast? Why or why not? (Some have legitimate medical reasons for not fasting.) What are some reasons for fasting today? Do you need to set apart a day or two to humble yourself and seek the face of God?

_____

_____

_____

THURSDAY: IT'S SHOWTIME!

1. Reread this week's segment of the biblical text. How do you see God's sovereignty at work? List ways.

_____

_____

_____

2. How do you see human responsibility at work? List ways.

_____

_____

_____

_____

3. What is the king's initial response to Esther (5:2–3)?

_____

_____

_____

_____

4. What is his later response to her (5:6; 7:2)?

_____

_____

_____

_____

5. What all did Haman, by his own admission, have going for him (5:9–13)?

_____

_____

_____

_____

_____

> Rulers used "I will give you your request—up to half the kingdom" as a euphemism for "I'm favorably predisposed to grant your request." It was not to be taken literally by those to whom it was said. (See also Mark 6:21–26.)

6. Were all Haman's blessings enough to make him content? Why or why not?

_____

_____

_____

_____

7. What is Haman's response to his wife's suggestion to build a seven-and-a-half-story gallows for impaling Mordecai? (See 5:14.)

_____

_____

8. Summarize how each of these couplings are portrayed in the Book of Esther:

A. King Ahasuerus and Queen Vashti

_____

_____

_____

B. Esther and Mordecai

_____

_____

_____

C. Haman and Zeresh

_____

_____

_____

FRIDAY: KING OF KINGS

1. Proverbs 21:1 tells us "The king's heart is in the hand of the Lord like channels of water; he turns it wherever he wants." What do you think this means? Does it apply to bosses and politicians and world leaders, as well?

_____

_____

_____

2. Ezra 1:1–4 says this:

> In the first year of King Cyrus of Persia, in order to fulfill the Lord's message spoken through Jeremiah, the Lord stirred the mind of King Cyrus of Persia. He disseminated a proclamation throughout all his kingdom, announcing in a written edict the following:

> So says King Cyrus of Persia: "The Lord God of heaven has given me all the kingdoms of the earth. He has instructed me to build a temple for him in Jerusalem, which is in Judah. **1:3** Anyone from his people among you (may his God be with him!) may go up to Jerusalem, which is in Judah, and may build the temple of the Lord God of Israel—he is the God who is in Jerusalem. **1:4** Let anyone who survives in any of those places where he is a resident foreigner be helped by his neighbors with silver, gold, equipment, and animals, along with voluntary offerings for the temple of God which is in Jerusalem."

What does this tell you about the extent of God's sovereignty?

_____

_____

_____

3. Nehemiah 2:1–9 says this:

> **Nehemiah 2:1** Then in the month of Nisan, in the twentieth year of King Artaxerxes, when wine was brought to me, I took the wine and gave it to the king. Previously I had not been depressed in the king's presence. **2:2** So the king said to me, "Why do you appear to be depressed when you aren't sick? What can this be other than sadness of heart?" This made me very fearful.

> I replied to the king, "O king, live forever! Why would I not be dejected in appearance when the city with the graves of my ancestors lies desolate and its gates destroyed by fire?" **2:4** The king responded, "What is it you are seeking?" Then I quickly prayed to the God of heaven **2:5** and said to the king, "If the king is so inclined and if your servant has found favor in your sight, dispatch me to Judah, to the city with the graves of my ancestors, so that I can rebuild it." **2:6** Then the king, with his consort sitting beside him, replied, "How long would your trip take, and when would you return?" Since the king was amenable to dispatching me, I gave him

a time. **2:7** I said to the king, "If the king is so inclined, let him give me letters for the governors of Trans-Euphrates that will enable me to travel safely until I reach Judah, **2:8** and a letter for Asaph the keeper of the king's nature preserve, so that he will give me timber for beams for the gates of the fortress adjacent to the temple and for the wall of the city and for the home to which I go." So the king granted me these provisions, for the good hand of my God was on me. **2:9** Then I went to the governors of Trans-Euphrates, and I presented to them the letters from the king. The king had sent with me officers of the army and horsemen.

What does this tell you about the extent of God's sovereignty?

_____

_____

_____

_____

4. Read Daniel 2—5:

Daniel 2

2:1 In the second year of his reign Nebuchadnezzar had many dreams. His mind was disturbed and he suffered from insomnia. **2:2** The king issued an order to summon the magicians, astrologers, sorcerers, and wise men in order to explain his dreams to him. So they came and awaited the king's instructions.

2:3 The king told them, "I have had a dream, and I am anxious to understand the dream." **2:4** The wise men replied to the king: [What follows is in Aramaic] "O king, live forever! Tell your servants the dream, and we will disclose its interpretation." **2:5** The king replied to the wise men, "My decision is firm. If you do not inform me of both the dream and its interpretation, you will be dismembered and your homes reduced to rubble! **2:6** But if you can disclose the dream and its interpretation, you will receive from me gifts, a reward, and considerable honor. So disclose to me the dream and its interpretation!" **2:7** They again replied, "Let the king inform us of the dream; then we will disclose its interpretation." **2:8** The king replied, "I know for sure that you are attempting to gain time, because you see that my decision is firm. **2:9** If you don't inform me of the dream, there is only one thing that is going to happen to you. For you have agreed among yourselves to report to me something false and deceitful until such time as things might change. So tell me the dream, and I will have confidence that you can disclose its interpretation."

2:10 The wise men replied to the king, "There is no man on earth who is able to disclose the king's secret, for no king, regardless of his position and power, has ever requested such a thing from any magician, astrologer, or wise man. **2:11** What the king is asking is too difficult, and no one exists who can disclose it to the king, except for the gods—but they don't live among mortals!"

2:12 Because of this the king got furiously angry and gave orders to destroy all the wise men of Babylon. **2:13** So a decree went out, and the wise men were about to be executed. Then Daniel and his friends were sought so that they could be executed.

2:14 Then Daniel spoke with prudent counsel to Arioch, who was in charge of the king's executioners and who had gone out to execute the wise men of Babylon. **2:15** He inquired of the king's deputy "Why is the decree from the king so urgent?" Then Arioch informed Daniel about the matter. **2:16** So Daniel went in and requested the king to grant him time, that he might disclose the interpretation to the king. **2:17** Then Daniel went to his home and informed his friends Hananiah, Mishael, and Azariah of the matter. **2:18** He asked them to pray for mercy from the God of heaven concerning this mystery so that he and his friends would not be destroyed with the rest of the wise men of Babylon. **2:19** Then in a night vision the mystery was revealed to Daniel. So Daniel praised the God of heaven, **2:20** saying, "Let the name of God be praised forever and ever, for wisdom and power belong to him.

2:21 He changes times and seasons, deposing some kings and establishing others. He gives wisdom to the wise; he imparts knowledge to those with understanding;

2:22 he reveals deep and hidden things. He knows what is in the darkness, and light resides with him.

2:23 O God of my fathers, I acknowledge and glorify you, for you have bestowed wisdom and power on me. Now you have enabled me to understand what I requested from you. For you have enabled me to understand the king's dilemma."

2:24 Then Daniel went in to see Arioch (whom the king had appointed to destroy the wise men of Babylon). He came and said to him, "Don't destroy the wise men of Babylon! Escort me to the king, and I will disclose the interpretation to him!"

2:25 So Arioch quickly ushered Daniel into the king's presence and said to him, "I have found a man from the captives of Judah who can make known the interpretation to the king." **2:26** The king then asked Daniel (whose name was also Belteshazzar), "Are you able to make known to me the dream that I saw, as well as its interpretation?" **2:27** Daniel replied to the king, "The mystery that the king is asking about is such that no wise men, astrologers, magicians, or diviners are able to disclose it to the king. **2:28** However, there is a God in heaven who reveals mysteries, and he has made known to King Nebuchadnezzar what will happen in the latter times. The dream and the visions you had on your bed are as follows.

2:29 "As for you, O king, while you were lying on your bed your thoughts turned to future things. The revealer of mysteries has made known to you what will take place. **2:30** As for me, this mystery was revealed to me not because I possess more wisdom than is in any other living person, but so that the king may understand the interpretation and comprehend the thoughts of your mind.

2:31 "You, O king, were watching as a great statue—one of impressive size and extraordinary brightness—was standing before you. Its appearance caused alarm. **2:32** As for that statue, its head was of fine gold, its chest and arms were of silver, its belly and thighs were of bronze. **2:33** Its legs were of iron; its feet were partly of iron and partly of clay. **2:34** You were watching as a stone was cut out but not by human hands. It struck the statue on its iron and clay feet, breaking them in pieces. **2:35** Then the iron, clay, bronze, silver, and gold were broken in pieces without distinction and became like chaff from the summer threshing floors that the wind carries away. Not a trace of them could be found. But the stone that struck the statue became a large mountain that filled the entire earth. **2:36** This was the dream. Now we will set forth before the king its interpretation.

2:37 "You, O king, are the king of kings. The God of heaven has granted you sovereignty, power, strength, and honor. **2:38** Wherever human beings, wild animals, and birds of the sky live—he has given them into your power. He has given you authority over them all. You are the head of gold. **2:39** Now after you there will arise another kingdom, one inferior to yours. Then a third kingdom, one of bronze, will rule in all the earth. **2:40** Then there will be a fourth kingdom, one strong like iron. Just like iron breaks in pieces and shatters everything, and as iron breaks in pieces all of these metals, so it will break in pieces and crush the others. **2:41** In that you were seeing feet and toes partly of wet clay and partly of iron, so this will be a divided kingdom. Some of the strength of iron will be in it, for you saw iron mixed with wet clay. **2:42** In that the toes of the feet were partly of iron and partly of clay, the latter stages of this kingdom will be partly strong and partly fragile. **2:43** And in that you saw iron mixed with wet clay, so people will be mixed with one another without adhering to one another, just as iron does not mix with clay. **2:44** In the days of those kings the God of heaven will raise up an everlasting kingdom that will not be destroyed and a kingdom that will not be left to another people. It will break in pieces and bring about the demise of all these kingdoms. But it will stand forever. **2:45** You saw that a stone was cut from a mountain, but not by human hands; it smashed the iron, bronze, clay, silver, and gold into pieces. The great God has made known to the king what will occur in the future. The dream is certain, and its interpretation is reliable."

2:46 Then king Nebuchadnezzar bowed down with his face to the ground and paid homage to Daniel. He gave orders to offer sacrifice and incense to him. **2:47** The king replied to Daniel, "Certainly your God is a God of gods and Lord of kings and revealer of mysteries, for you were able to reveal this mystery!" **2:48** Then the king elevated Daniel to high position and bestowed on him many marvelous gifts. He granted him authority over the entire province of Babylon and made him the main prefect over all the wise men of Babylon. **2:49** And at Daniel's request, the king appointed Shadrach, Meshach, and Abednego over the administration of the province of Babylon. Daniel himself served in the king's court.

Daniel 3

3:1 King Nebuchadnezzar had a golden statue made. It was ninety feet tall and nine feet wide. He erected it on the plain of Dura in the province of Babylon. **3:2** Then King Nebuchadnezzar sent out a summons to assemble the satraps, prefects, governors, counselors, treasurers, judges, magistrates, and all the other authorities of the province to attend the dedication of the statue that he had erected. **3:3** So the satraps, prefects, governors, counselors, treasurers, judges, magistrates, and all the other provincial authorities assembled for the dedication of the statue that King Nebuchadnezzar had erected. They were standing in front of the statue that Nebuchadnezzar had erected.

3:4 Then the herald made a loud proclamation: "To you, O peoples, nations, and language groups, the following command is given: **3:5** When you hear the sound of the horn, flute, zither, trigon, harp, pipes, and all kinds of music, you must bow down and pay homage to the golden statue that King Nebuchadnezzar has erected. **3:6** Whoever does not bow down and pay homage will immediately be thrown into the midst of a furnace of blazing fire!" **3:7** Therefore when they all heard the sound of the horn, flute, zither, trigon, harp, pipes, and all kinds of music, all the peoples, nations, and language groups began bowing down and paying homage to the golden statue that King Nebuchadnezzar had erected.

3:8 So at that time certain Chaldeans came forward and brought malicious accusations against the Jews. **3:9** They said to King Nebuchadnezzar, "O king, live forever! **3:10** You have issued an edict, O king, that everyone must bow down and pay homage to the golden statue when they hear the sound of the horn, flute, zither, trigon, harp, pipes, and all kinds of music. **3:11** And whoever does not bow down and pay homage must be thrown into the midst of a furnace of blazing fire. **3:12** But there are Jewish men whom you appointed over the administration of the province of Babylon—Shadrach, Meshach, and Abednego—and these men have not shown proper respect to you, O king. They don't serve your gods and they don't pay homage to the golden statue that you have erected."

3:13 Then Nebuchadnezzar in a fit of rage demanded that they bring Shadrach, Meshach, and Abednego before him. So they brought them before the king. **3:14** Nebuchadnezzar said to them, "Is it true, Shadrach, Meshach, and Abednego, that you don't serve my gods and that you don't pay homage to the golden statue that I erected? **3:15** Now if you are ready, when you hear the sound of the horn, flute, zither, trigon, harp, pipes, and all kinds of music, you must bow down and pay homage to the statue that I had made. If you don't pay homage to it, you will immediately be thrown into the midst of the furnace of blazing fire. Now, who is that god who can rescue you from my power?" **3:16** Shadrach, Meshach, and Abednego replied to King Nebuchadnezzar, "We do not need to give you a reply concerning this. **3:17** If our God whom we are serving exists, he is able to rescue us from the furnace of blazing fire, and he will rescue us, O king, from your power as well. **3:18** But if not, let it be known to you, O king, that we don't serve your gods, and we will not pay homage to the golden statue that you have erected."

3:19 Then Nebuchadnezzar was filled with rage, and his disposition changed toward Shadrach, Meshach, and Abednego. He gave orders to heat the furnace seven times hotter than it was normally heated. **3:20** He ordered strong soldiers in his army to tie up

Shadrach, Meshach, and Abednego and to throw them into the furnace of blazing fire. **3:21** Then those men were bound, while still wearing their cloaks, trousers, turbans, and other clothes, and were thrown into the midst of the furnace of blazing fire. **3:22** But since the king's command was so urgent, and the furnace was so excessively hot, the men who escorted Shadrach, Meshach, and Abednego were killed by the fiery flame. **3:23** But those three men, Shadrach, Meshach, and Abednego, fell into the midst of the furnace of blazing fire while securely bound.

3:24 Then King Nebuchadnezzar was startled and quickly got up. He said to his ministers, "Wasn't it three men that we tied up and threw into the fire?" They replied to the king, "For sure, O king." **3:25** He answered, "But I see four men, untied and walking around in the midst of the fire! No harm has come to them! And the appearance of the fourth is like that of a god!" **3:26** Then Nebuchadnezzar approached the door of the furnace of blazing fire. He called out, "Shadrach, Meshach, and Abednego, servants of the most high God, come out! Come here!" Then Shadrach, Meshach, and Abednego emerged from the midst of the fire. **3:27** Once the satraps, prefects, governors, and ministers of the king had gathered around, they saw that those men were physically unharmed by the fire. The hair of their heads was not singed, nor were their trousers damaged. Not even the smell of fire was to be found on them!

3:28 Nebuchadnezzar exclaimed, "Praised be the God of Shadrach, Meshach, and Abednego, who has sent forth his angel and has rescued his servants who trusted in him, ignoring the edict of the king and giving up their bodies rather than serve or pay homage to any god other than their God! **3:29** I hereby decree that any people, nation, or language group that blasphemes the god of Shadrach, Meshach, or Abednego will be dismembered and his home reduced to rubble. For there exists no other god who can deliver in this way." **3:30** Then Nebuchadnezzar promoted Shadrach, Meshach, and Abednego in the province of Babylon.

Daniel 4

4:1 "King Nebuchadnezzar, to all peoples, nations, and language groups that live in all the land: Best wishes! **4:2** I am delighted to tell you about the signs and wonders that the most high God has done for me.

4:3 "How great are his signs! How mighty are his wonders! His kingdom will last forever, and his authority continues from one generation to the next."

4:4 I, Nebuchadnezzar, was at ease in my home, living luxuri-ously in my palace. **4:5** I saw a dream that scared me. The things I imagined while lying on my bed—these visions of my mind—were terrifying me. **4:6** So I issued an order for all the wise men of Babylon to be brought before me so that they could make known to me the interpretation of the dream. **4:7** When the magicians, astrologers, wise men, and diviners entered, I recounted the dream for them. But they were unable to make known its interpretation to me. **4:8** Later Daniel entered (whose name is Belteshazzar after the name of my god, and in whom there is a spirit of the holy gods). I recounted the dream for him as well, **4:9** saying, "Belteshazzar, chief of the magicians, in whom I know there to be a spirit of the holy gods and whom no mystery baffles, consider my dream that I saw and set forth its interpretation! **4:10** Here are the visions of my mind while I was on my bed. While I was watching, there was a tree in the midst of the land. It was enormously tall.

4:11 The tree grew large and strong. Its top reached far into the sky; it could be seen from the borders of all the land.

4:12 Its foliage was attractive and its fruit plentiful; on it there was food enough for all. Under it the wild animals used to seek shade, and in its branches the birds of the sky used to nest. All crea-tures used to feed themselves from it.

4:13 While I was watching in my mind's visions on my bed, a holy sentinel came down from heaven.

4:14 He called out loudly as follows: 'Chop down the tree and lop off its branches! Strip off its foliage and scatter its fruit! Let the animals flee from under it and the birds from its branches!

4:15 But leave its taproot in the ground, with a band of iron and bronze around it surrounded by the grass of the field. Let it become damp with the dew of the sky, and let it live with the ani-mals in the grass of the land.

4:16 Let his mind be altered from that of a human being, and let an animal's mind be given to him, and let seven periods of time go by for him.

4:17 This announcement is by the decree of the sentinels; this decision is by the pronouncement of the holy ones, so that those who are alive may understand that the Most High has authority over human kingdoms, and he bestows them on whomever he wishes. He establishes over them even the lowliest of human beings.'

4:18 "This is the dream that I, King Nebuchadnezzar, saw. Now you, Belteshazzar, declare its interpretation, for none of the wise men in my kingdom are able to make known to me the interpretation. But you can do so, for a spirit of the holy gods is in you."

4:19 Then Daniel (whose name is also Belteshazzar) was briefly upset; his thoughts were alarming him. The king said, "Belteshazzar, don't let the dream and its interpretation alarm you." But Belteshazzar replied, "Sir, if only the dream were for your enemies and its interpretation applied to your adversaries! **4:20** The tree that you saw that grew large and strong, whose top reached to the sky, and which could be seen in all the land, **4:21** whose foliage was attractive and its fruit plentiful, and from which there was food available for all, under whose branches wild animals used to live, and in whose branches birds of the sky used to nest— **4:22** it is you, O king! For you have become great and strong. Your greatness is such that it reaches to heaven, and your authority to the ends of the earth. **4:23** As for the king seeing a holy sentinel coming down from heaven and saying, 'Chop down the tree and destroy it. But leave its taproot in the ground, with a band of iron and bronze around it, surrounded by the grass of the field. Let it become damp with the dew of the sky, and let it live with the wild animals, until seven periods of time go by for him'—

4:24 "This is the interpretation, O king. It is the decision of the Most High that this has happened to my lord the king. **4:25** You will be driven from human society, and you will live with the wild animals. You will be fed grass like oxen, and you will become damp with the dew of the sky. Seven periods of time will pass by for you, before you understand that the Most High is ruler over human kingdoms and gives them to whomever he wishes. **4:26** They said to leave the taproot of the tree, for your kingdom will be restored to you when you come to understand that heaven rules. **4:27** Therefore, O king, may my advice be pleasing to you. Break away from your sins by doing what is right, and from your iniquities by showing mercy to the poor. Perhaps your prosperity will be prolonged."

4:28 Now all of this happened to King Nebuchadnezzar. **4:29** After twelve months, he happened to be walking around on the walls of the royal palace of Babylon. **4:30** The king uttered these words: "Is this not the great Babylon that I have built for a royal residence by my own mighty strength and for my majestic honor?" **4:31** While these words were still on the king's lips, a voice came down from heaven: "It is hereby announced to you, King Nebuchadnezzar, that your kingdom has been removed from you! **4:32** You will be driven from human society, and you will live with the wild animals. You will be fed grass like oxen, and seven periods of time will pass by for you before you understand that the Most High is ruler over human kingdoms and gives them to whomever he wishes."

4:33 Now in that very moment this pronouncement about Nebuchadnezzar came true. He was driven from human society, he ate grass like oxen, and his body became damp with the dew of the sky, until his hair became long like an eagle's feathers, and his nails like a bird's claws.

4:34 But at the end of the appointed time I, Nebuchadnezzar, looked up toward heaven, and my sanity returned to me. I extolled the Most High, and I praised and glorified the one who lives forever. For his authority is an everlasting authority, and his kingdom extends from one generation to the next.

4:35 All the inhabitants of the earth are regarded as nothing. He does as he wishes with the army of heaven and with those who inhabit the earth. No one slaps his hand and says to him, 'What have you done?'

4:36 At that time my sanity returned to me. I was restored to the honor of my kingdom, and my splendor returned to me. My ministers and my nobles were seeking me out, and I was reinstated over my kingdom. I became even greater than before. **4:37** Now I, Nebuchadnezzar, praise and exalt and glorify the King of heaven, for all his deeds are right and his ways are just. He is able to bring down those who live in pride.

Daniel 5

5:1 King Belshazzar prepared a great banquet for a thousand of his nobles, and he was drinking wine in front of them all. **5:2** While under the influence of the wine, Belshazzar issued an order to bring in the gold and silver vessels—the ones that Nebuchadnezzar his father had confiscated from the temple in Jerusalem—so that the king and his nobles, together with his wives and his concubines, could drink from them. **5:3** So they brought the gold and silver vessels that had been confiscated from the temple, the house of God in Jerusalem, and the king and his nobles, together with his wives and concubines, drank from them. **5:4** As they drank wine, they praised the gods of gold and silver, bronze, iron, wood, and stone.

5:5 At that very moment the fingers of a human hand appeared and wrote on the plaster of the royal palace wall, opposite the lampstand. The king was watching the back of the hand that was writing. **5:6** Then all the color drained from the king's face and he became alarmed. The joints of his hips gave way, and his knees began knocking together. **5:7** The king called out loudly to summon the astrologers, wise men, and diviners. The king proclaimed to the wise men of Babylon that anyone who could read this inscription and disclose its interpretation would be clothed in purple and have a golden collar placed on his neck and be third ruler in the kingdom.

5:8 So all the king's wise men came in, but they were unable to read the writing or to make known its interpretation to the king. **5:9** Then King Belshazzar was very terrified, and he was visibly shaken. His nobles were completely dumbfounded.

5:10 Due to the noise caused by the king and his nobles, the queen mother then entered the banquet room. She said, "O king, live forever! Don't be alarmed! Don't be shaken! **5:11** There is a man in your kingdom who has within him a spirit of the holy gods. In the days of your father, he proved to have insight, discernment, and wisdom like that of the gods. King Nebuchadnezzar your father appointed him chief of the magicians, astrologers, wise men, and diviners. **5:12** Thus there was found in this man Daniel, whom the king renamed Belteshazzar, an extraordinary spirit, knowledge, and skill to interpret dreams, solve riddles, and decipher knotty problems. Now summon Daniel, and he will disclose the interpretation."

5:13 So Daniel was brought in before the king. The king said to Daniel, "Are you that Daniel who is one of the captives of Judah, whom my father the king brought from Judah? **5:14** I have heard about you, how there is a spirit of the gods in you, and how you have insight, discernment, and extraordinary wisdom. **5:15** Now the wise men and astrologers were brought before me to read this writing and make known to me its interpretation. But they were unable to disclose the interpretation of the message. **5:16** However, I have heard that you are able to provide interpretations and to decipher knotty problems. Now if you are able to read this writing and make known to me its interpretation, you will wear purple and have a golden collar around your neck and be third ruler in the kingdom."

5:17 But Daniel replied to the king, "Keep your gifts and give your rewards to someone else. However, I will read the writing for the king and make known its interpretation. **5:18** As for you, O king, the most high God bestowed on Nebuchadnezzar your father a kingdom, greatness, honor, and majesty. **5:19** Due to the greatness that he bestowed on him, all peoples, nations, and language groups were trembling with fear before him. He killed whom he wished, he spared whom he wished, he exalted whom he wished, and he brought low whom he wished. **5:20** And when his mind became arrogant and his spirit filled with pride, he was deposed from his royal throne and his honor was removed from him. **5:21** He was driven from human society, his mind was changed to that of an animal, he lived with the wild donkeys, he was fed grass like oxen, and his body became damp with the dew of the sky, until he came to understand that the most high God rules over human kingdoms, and he appoints over them whomever he wishes.

5:22 "But you, his son Belshazzar, have not humbled yourself, although you knew all this. **5:23** Instead, you have exalted yourself against the Lord of heaven. You brought before you the vessels from his temple, and you and your nobles, together with your wives and concubines, drank wine from them. You praised the gods of silver, gold, bronze, iron, wood, and stone—gods that cannot see or hear or comprehend! But you have not glorified the God who has in his control your very breath and all your ways! **5:24** Therefore the palm of a hand was sent from him, and this writing was inscribed.

5:25 "This is the writing that was inscribed: MENE, MENE, TEQEL, and PHARSIN. **5:26** This is the interpretation of the words: As for *mene*—God has numbered your kingdom's days and brought it to an end. **5:27** As for *teqel*—you are weighed on the balances and found to be lacking. **5:28** As for *peres*—your kingdom is divided and given over to the Medes and Persians."

5:29 Then, on Belshazzar's orders, Daniel was clothed in purple, a golden collar was placed around his neck, and he was proclaimed third ruler in the kingdom. **5:30** And in that very night Belshazzar, the Babylonian king, was killed. **5:31** So Darius the Mede took control of the kingdom when he was about sixty-two years old.

5. After reading this, summarize what God controls in the universe:

_____

_____

_____

_____

6. Now that you have a global picture, let's get specific. List key relationships, jobs, locations and/or circumstances in your life. How might God use you where you are "for such a time as this"?

_____

_____

_____

7. Make a private list of your own flaws. Pray through them, asking God for the grace to turn them into strengths.

_____

_____

_____

SATURDAY: HE IS ABLE

Esther and Mordecai were reluctant heroes. We could write multiple reasons why they were not ideal candidates for God's "Whom shall I use?" list. Yet in the end, they chose the path of courage, and He worked mightily through them. Or perhaps it's the other way around—He worked mightily and they chose the path of courage. Maybe it's a combination of both.

There are many reasons God shouldn't use *us*. Yet we're in good company.

Noah got drunk.
Abraham lied about his wife.
Jacob was a swindler.
Moses stuttered.
He also had a short fuse.
Miriam was a gossip.
Gideon put God to the test.
Naomi was a widow.
Sarah was too old.

David was too young.

David committed adultery.

Solomon had a bunch of wives.

Elijah got burnt out.

Hosea married a prostitute.

Jonah ran away from God.

Jeremiah got depressed.

The woman at the well had been dumped by five husbands.[5]

Martha was too busy.

Lazarus was dead.

Thomas doubted.

Peter was afraid of death.

John Mark was rejected by the apostle Paul.

Timothy had stomach problems.

Moses was a murderer.

So was David.

So was Paul.

"But we have this treasure in jars of clay to show that this all-surpassing power is from God and not from us" (2 Corinthians 4:7).

What obstacles keep you from total surrender to the Lord and His will? Do you think you could never measure up? Is your past too awful? Are you too weak? Are you imperfect?

A pastor friend bought a plain-looking urn during a trip to the Middle East. He put candy inside and during a church service back home he invited the children to come forward to get some. Not one of the kids gave the urn itself any thought. They were too focused on the treasure inside.

When we walk in the Spirit, our lives are like that. What's inside is so radiant that people see beyond us to Him. And if you feel weak, you're in the ideal situation for God to show his all-surpassing power through you. Humble yourself before Him. Yes, you are a mere "clay pot." But you can show forth the treasure inside.

Prayer: *Heavenly Father, I need You! I am weak, but You are strong. Forgive the pride that keeps me from coming to You. Make me what You want me to be. What would You have me do, Lord? I offer You*

---

[5] During the time of Christ's earthly ministry, women typically didn't divorce their husbands. Husbands divorced their wives.

my time, my talents, and my resources. And I offer You my past sins and all my weaknesses. Give me wisdom to know how best to use it all for Your glory. Help me never to compare myself to others. Show Your perfect strength through my weakness. Thank You for the treasure of Your Spirit. In the name of Your Son I pray, Amen.

For Memorization: "Don't imagine that because you are part of the king's household you will be the one Jew who will escape. If you keep quiet at this time, liberation and protection for the Jews will appear from another source, while you and your father's household perish. It may very well be that you have achieved royal status for such a time as this!" (Esth. 4:14).

WEEK 5 OF 5

All's Well That Ends Well: Esther 6—10

Scripture: The king asked, "What great honor was bestowed on Mordecai because of this?" The king's attendants who served him responded, "Not a thing was done for him." (Esther 6:3)

The construction of the Book of Esther receives praise from the best of literary minds. For lovers of English literature, this book is a great place to start when seeking introduction to the Bible. The author uses humor, repetition, irony, and contrast masterfully.

Some literature teachers use Esther as an example of a "Cinderella story." Because the name of God appears nowhere in the book, Esther is often welcomed in nonreligious contexts where a more obviously theological story would be excluded. As our world grows ever more secular, the book itself is perhaps "for such a time as this."

At the start of our study of Esther, we considered the need to read the entire story before drawing application from the biblical text. Well, now we've read and studied the whole story. So what has God said through this ancient work that we can apply to our lives in the twenty-first century? Let's start with some observations:

- Number of times God is mentioned in Esther: 0
- Number of times prayer is mentioned in Esther: 0
- Number of times the temple or Jerusalem are mentioned in Esther: 0
- Number of times God's purposes are thwarted in Esther: 0

How do we interpret this?

The first thing we learn from Esther is that God is in control, even though He's invisible.

A king forgets to honor someone who has saved his life. That is, until the perfect time—God's time—the moment when it is most necessary for the overlooked man to find favor. And ultimately a young woman and her cousin, unobservant religiously, are used to keep an entire nation from annihilation. The story of God's sovereignty unfolds without ever mentioning God's name.

We've seen sovereignty emphasized elsewhere in scripture. Think of the Book of Job. In it we read how the righteous Job lost children, home, business, health—everything but a wife who urged him to curse God. And God never told Job why. He just gave him a quiz that included such questions as, "Where were you when I laid the foundation of the earth (38:4)?" and "Have you ever in your life commanded the morning?" (38:12). The only appropriate answer is silence, trembling, and awe.

I had been contemplating such thoughts this week when my sister called to tell me about her friend, Angie. Angie had wanted to be married in her twenties, but she'd waited for the right guy. So eighteen months ago, at age forty, she had finally said "I do." My sister and her daughters had flown fifteen hundred miles to celebrate with Angie. But then there was this call. There had been a car accident. Coming back from taking his mom to lunch—headed to a school to read to a class full of kids—Angie's husband was killed. A county sheriff, a good guy, gone.

Often, despite all we know of God, things happen that don't seem to make sense—things that make it look like the world is spinning out of control. Things that break our hearts. We all have such stories, don't we? The tsunami, the earthquake, the hurricane, the war, the sickness. Our planet groans as if writhing in childbirth as it longs for the day when the Prince on a white horse will arrive and make all things new. But this is not that day. So for now, like Jesus at Lazarus' tomb knowing a happy ending is right around the corner, we still weep.

We learn from the Book of Esther that it may look like all is lost. It may seem as though God is absent. Yet the known facts are not all the facts. The story isn't over yet.

So we wait and trust.

The second thing we learn from Esther is that God keeps His promises to His people.

Way back in the events recorded in Genesis, God promised Abram that He would make of him a great nation. Later He promised David an eternal throne. And God kept His promises. He did so even when His people blended so well with the culture that no one would have guessed they were His.

One day the focus of God's big program will revert to Israel. Yet for a time the Church, the Body of Christ, is at the center. Believers in Jesus Christ have been "grafted into the tree" as it were, so we are included in an illustrious group of those who can call God "Father." As such, we are the recipients of spiritual blessings galore.

God promised something to the nation of Israel that He also promises to us: His presence. He told Abraham, "I will be with you" as Abraham set out to find the new land (Gen. 26:3). God said the same to Jacob (31:3) and to Joseph (48:21) and to Moses (Ex. 3:12) and to Joshua (Deut. 31:23; Josh. 1:5). Add Gideon and Solomon. Indeed, He promised His presence to the entire nation (Isa. 43:2). And we have that same promise: "I will never leave you, nor will I ever forsake you" (Heb. 13:5).

Does God keep His promises? Yes.

Will He abandon us? No.

Even if we're imperfect? Even if we're imperfect.

The Book of Esther tells us God keeps His promise through any means possible regardless of what anyone else is doing. And He has promised never to leave.

We are never alone.

MONDAY: THE BIG PICTURE

1. Ask God to give you insight through His Spirit. Then read Esther chapters six through ten.

Esther 6:1 Throughout that night the king was unable to sleep, so he asked for the book containing the historical records to be brought. As the records were being read in the king's presence, **6:2** it was found written that Mordecai had disclosed that Bigthan and Teresh, two of the king's eunuchs who guarded the entrance, had plotted to assassinate King Ahasuerus.

6:3 The king asked, "What great honor was bestowed on Mordecai because of this?" The king's attendants who served him responded, "Not a thing was done for him."

6:4 Then the king said, "Who is that in the courtyard?" Now Haman had come to the outer courtyard of the palace to suggest that the king hang Mordecai on the gallows that he had constructed for him. **6:5** The king's attendants said to him, "It is Haman who is standing in the courtyard." The king said, "Let him enter."

6:6 So Haman came in, and the king said to him, "What should be done for the man whom the king wishes to honor?" Haman thought to himself, "Who is it that the king would want to honor more than me?" **6:7** So Haman said to the king, "For the man whom the king wishes to honor, **6:8** let them bring royal attire which the king himself has worn and a horse on which the king himself has ridden—one bearing the royal insignia! **6:9** Then let this clothing and this horse be given to one of the king's noble officials. Let him then clothe the man whom the king wishes to honor, and let him lead him about through the plaza of the city on the horse, calling before him, 'So shall it be done to the man whom the king wishes to honor!'"

6:10 The king then said to Haman, "Go quickly! Take the clothing and the horse, just as you have described, and do as you just indicated to Mordecai the Jew who sits at the king's gate. Don't neglect a single thing of all that you have said."

6:11 So Haman took the clothing and the horse, and he clothed Mordecai. He led him about on the horse throughout the plaza of the city, calling before him, "So shall it be done to the man whom the king wishes to honor!"

6:12 Then Mordecai again sat at the king's gate, while Haman hurried away to his home, mournful and with a veil over his head. **6:13** Haman then related to his wife Zeresh and to all his friends everything that had happened to him. These wise men, along with his wife Zeresh, said to him, "If indeed this Mordecai before whom you have begun to fall is Jewish, you will not be adequate for him. No, you will surely fall before him!"

6:14 While they were still speaking with him, the king's eunuchs arrived. They quickly brought Haman to the banquet that Esther had prepared.

Esther 7

7:1 So the king and Haman came to dine with Queen Esther. **7:2** On the second day of the banquet of wine the king asked Esther, "What is your request, Queen Esther? It shall be granted to you. And what is your petition? Ask up to half the kingdom, and it shall be done!"

7:3 Queen Esther replied, "If I have met with your approval, O king, and if the king is so inclined, grant me my life as my request, and my people as my petition. **7:4** For we have been sold—both I and my people—to destruction and to slaughter and to annihilation! If we had simply been sold as male and female slaves, I would have remained silent, for such distress would not have been sufficient for troubling the king."

7:5 Then King Ahasuerus responded to Queen Esther, "Who is this individual? Where is this person to be found who is presumptuous enough to act in this way?"

7:6 Esther replied, "The oppressor and enemy is this evil Haman!" Then Haman became terrified in the presence of the king and queen. **7:7** In rage the king arose from the banquet of wine and withdrew to the palace garden. Meanwhile, Haman stood to beg Esther the queen for his life, for he realized that the king had now determined a catastrophic end for him.

7:8 When the king returned from the palace garden to the banquet of wine, Haman was throwing himself down on the couch where Esther was lying. The king exclaimed, "Will he also attempt to rape the queen while I am still in the building!" As these words left the king's mouth, they covered Haman's face. **7:9** Harbona, one of the king's eunuchs, said, "Indeed, there is the gallows that Haman made for Mordecai, who spoke out in the king's behalf. It stands near Haman's home and is seventy-five feet high. The king said, "Hang him on it!" **7:10** So they hanged Haman on the very gallows that he had prepared for Mordecai. The king's rage then abated.

Esther 8

8:1 On that same day King Ahasuerus gave the estate of Haman, that adversary of the Jews, to Queen Esther. Now Mordecai had come before the king, for Esther had revealed how he was related to her. **8:2** The king then removed his signet ring (the very one he had taken back from Haman) and gave it to Mordecai. And Esther designated Mordecai to be in charge of Haman's estate.

8:3 Then Esther again spoke with the king, falling at his feet. She wept and begged him for mercy, that he might nullify the evil of Haman the Agagite which he had intended against the Jews. **8:4** When the king extended to Esther the gold scepter, she arose and stood before the king.

8:5 She said, "If the king is so inclined and if I have met with his approval and if the matter is agreeable to the king and if I am attractive to him, let an edict be written rescinding those recorded intentions of Haman the son of Hammedatha, the Agagite, which he wrote in order to destroy the Jews who are throughout all the king's provinces. **8:6** For how can I watch the calamity that will befall my people, and how can I watch the destruction of my relatives?"

8:7 King Ahasuerus replied to Queen Esther and to Mordecai the Jew, "Look, I have already given Haman's estate to Esther, and he has been hanged on the gallows because he struck out against the Jews. **8:8** Now you write in the king's name whatever in your opinion is appropriate concerning the Jews and seal it with the king's signet ring. Any decree that is written in the king's name and sealed with the king's signet ring cannot be rescinded.

8:9 The king's scribes were quickly summoned—in the third month (that is, the month of Sivan), on the twenty-third day. They wrote out everything that Mordecai instructed to the Jews and to the satraps and the governors and the officials of the provinces all the way from India to Ethiopia—a hundred and twenty-seven provinces in all—to each province in its own script and to each people in their own language, and to the Jews according to their own script and their own language. **8:10** Mordecai wrote in the name of King Ahasuerus and sealed it with the king's signet ring. He then sent letters by couriers on horses, who rode royal horses that were very swift.

8:11 The king thereby allowed the Jews who were in every city to assemble and to stand up for themselves—to destroy, to kill, and to annihilate any army of whatever people or province that should become their adversaries, including their women and children, and to confiscate their property. **8:12** This was to take place on a certain day throughout all the provinces of King Ahasuerus—namely, on the thirteenth day of the twelfth month (that is, the month of Adar). **8:13** A copy of the edict was to be presented as law throughout each and every province and made known to all peoples, so that the Jews might be prepared on that day to avenge themselves from their enemies.

8:14 The couriers who were riding the royal horses went forth with the king's edict without delay. And the law was presented in Susa the citadel as well.

8:15 Now Mordecai went out from the king's presence in purple and white royal attire, with a large golden crown and a purple linen mantle. The city of Susa shouted with joy. **8:16** For the Jews there was radiant happiness and joyous honor. **8:17** Throughout every province and throughout every city where the king's edict and his law came, the Jews experienced happiness and joy, banquets and holidays. Many of the resident peoples pretended to be Jews, because the fear of the Jews had overcome them.

Esther 9

9:1 In the twelfth month (that is, the month of Adar), on its thirteenth day, the edict of the king and his law were to be executed. It was on this day that the enemies of the Jews had supposed that they would gain power over them. But contrary to expectations, the Jews gained power over their enemies. **9:2** The Jews assembled themselves in their cities throughout all the provinces of King Ahasuerus to strike out against those who were seeking their harm. No one was able to stand before them, for dread of them fell on all the peoples. **9:3** All the officials of the provinces, the satraps, the governors and those who performed the king's business were assisting the Jews, for the dread of Mordecai had fallen on them. **9:4** Mordecai was high ranking in the king's palace, and word about him was spreading throughout all the provinces. His influence continued to become greater and greater.

9:5 The Jews struck all their enemies with the sword, bringing death and destruction, and they did as they pleased with their enemies. **9:6** In Susa the citadel the Jews killed and destroyed five hundred men. **9:7** In addition, they also killed Parshandatha, Dalphon, Aspatha, **9:8** Poratha, Adalia, Aridatha, **9:9** Parmashta, Arisai, Aridai, and Vaizatha, **9:10** the ten sons of Haman son of Hammedatha, the enemy of the Jews. But they did not confiscate their property.

9:11 On that same day the number of those killed in Susa the citadel was brought to the king's attention. **9:12** Then the king said to Queen Esther, "In Susa the citadel the Jews have killed and destroyed five hundred men and the ten sons of Haman! What then have they done in the rest of the king's provinces? What is your request? It shall be given to you. What other petition do you have? It shall be done."

9:13 Esther replied, "If the king is so inclined, let the Jews who are in Susa be permitted to act tomorrow also according to today's law, and let them hang the ten sons of Haman on the gallows."

9:14 So the king issued orders for this to be done. A law was passed in Susa, and the ten sons of Haman were hanged. **9:15** The Jews who were in Susa then assembled on the fourteenth day of the month of Adar, and they killed three hundred men in Susa. But they did not confiscate their property.

9:16 The rest of the Jews who were throughout the provinces of the king assembled in order to stand up for themselves and to have rest from their enemies. They killed seventy-five thousand of their adversaries, but they did not confiscate their property. **9:17** All of this happened on the thirteenth day of the month of Adar. They then rested on the fourteenth day and made it a day for banqueting and happiness.

The Origins of the Feast of Purim

9:18 But the Jews who were in Susa assembled on the thirteenth and fourteenth days, and rested on the fifteenth, making it a day for banqueting and happiness. **9:19** This is why the Jews who are in the rural country—those who live in rural cities—set aside the fourteenth day of the month of Adar as a holiday for happiness, banqueting, holiday, and sending gifts to one another.

9:20 Mordecai wrote these matters down and sent letters to all the Jews who were throughout all the provinces of King Ahasuerus, both near and far, **9:21** to have them observe the fourteenth and the fifteenth day of the month of Adar each year **9:22** as the time when the Jews gave themselves rest from their enemies—the month when their trouble was turned to happiness and their mourning to a holiday. These were to be days of banqueting, happiness, sending gifts to one another, and providing for the poor.

9:23 So the Jews committed themselves to continue what they had begun to do and to what Mordecai had written to them. **9:24** For Haman the son of Hammedatha, the Agagite, the enemy of all the Jews, had devised plans against the Jews to destroy them. He had cast *pur* (that is, the lot) in order to afflict and destroy them. **9:25** But when the matter came to the king's attention, the king gave written orders that Haman's evil intentions that he had devised against the Jews should fall on his own head. He and his sons were hanged on the gallows. **9:26** For this reason these days are known as *Purim*, after the name of *pur*. **9:27** Therefore, because of the account found in this letter and what they had faced in this regard and what had happened to them, the Jews established as binding on themselves, their descendants, and all who joined their company that they should observe these two days without fail, just as written and at the appropriate time on an annual basis. **9:28** These days were to be remembered and to be celebrated in every generation and in every family, every province, and every city. The Jews were not to fail to observe these days of Purim; the remembrance of them was not to cease among their descendants.

9:29 So Queen Esther, the daughter of Abihail, and Mordecai the Jew wrote with full authority to confirm this second letter about Purim. **9:30** Letters were sent to all the Jews in the hundred and twenty-seven provinces of the empire of Ahasuerus—words of true peace— **9:31** to establish these days of Purim in their proper times, just as Mordecai the Jew and Queen Esther had established, and just as they had established both for themselves and their descendants, matters pertaining to fasting and lamentation. **9:32** Esther's command established these matters of Purim, and the matter was officially recorded.

Esther 10

10:1 King Ahasuerus then imposed forced labor on the land and on the coastlands of the sea. **10:2** Now all the actions carried out under his authority and his great achievements, along with an exact statement concerning the greatness of Mordecai, whom the king promoted, are they not written in the Book of the Chronicles of the Kings of Media and Persia? **10:3** Mordecai the Jew was second only to King Ahasuerus. He was the highest-ranking Jew, and he was admired by his numerous relatives. He worked enthusiastically for the good of his people and was an advocate for the welfare of all his descendants.

2. Summarize what happened.

_____

_____

_____

3. What events seem coincidental?

_____

_____

_____

4. The same God who weaved the events in Esther is sovereign in the lives of his children today. Write a short prayer, thanking God for orchestrating the seen and unseen events in your life.

_____

_____

_____

TUESDAY: PRIDE AND PREJUDICE

1. What can we discern about Haman's character through his response to the king's question (6:7–9)?

_____

_____

_____

2. Describe how you think Haman must have felt when he discovered Mordecai, his enemy, was to be honored with the very ceremony Haman had proposed for himself.

_____

_____

_____

3. How do Haman's wife and advisors interpret the events (6:12–14)? Why do you think they saw it that way?

_____

_____

_____

_____

4. Proverbs 16:18 tells us that pride goes before destruction. How has Haman's pride led to his own downfall?

_____

_____

_____

5. The Big Oversight

A. Read Esther 2:21—3:2 below.

> **Esther 2:21** In those days while Mordecai was sitting at the king's gate, Bigthan and Teresh, two of the king's eunuchs who protected the entrance, got angry and plotted to assassinate King Ahasuerus. **2:22** When Mordecai learned of the conspiracy, he informed Queen Esther, and Esther told the king in Mordecai's behalf. **2:23** The king then had the matter investigated and, finding it to be so, had the two conspirators hanged on a gallows. It was then recorded in the daily chronicles in the king's presence. **3:1** Sometime later King Ahasuerus promoted Haman the son of Hammedatha, the Agagite, exalting him and setting his position above that of all the officials who were with him. **3:2** As a result, all the king's servants who were at the king's gate were bowing and paying homage to Haman, for the king had so commanded. However, Mordecai did not bow, nor did he pay him homage.

B. Herodotus records that a log was kept of the king's benefactors. He tells of one man who was rewarded with a large estate for his service to the king.[6] What should have happened to Mordecai after he proved his loyalty to the king?

_____

_____

_____

_____

C. What happened instead? How do you think that made Mordecai feel?

_____

_____

_____

_____

D. Now that you know the whole story, what turned out for the good as a result of the king's failure to reward Mordecai in a timely manner?

_____

_____

_____

_____

E. What does this story suggest about God's timing?

_____

_____

_____

[6] Herodotus, *Histories,* 8.85

F. First Peter 5:5–7 says, "God opposes the proud but gives grace to the humble. And God will exalt you in due time, if you humble yourselves under his mighty hand by casting all your cares on him because he cares for you." Humble yourself before God, casting your cares on Him, offering Him your hurt feelings for times someone else received credit you deserved and trusting Him to exalt you when the time is right.

_____

_____

_____

_____

WEDNESDAY: SLEEPLESS IN SUSA

1. God has been at work bringing about the events recorded in this week's reading. He uses seemingly insignificant things—such as someone's sleepless night—to work out His plans. Tell of a time when God used something that seemed insignificant in your life for His purposes.

_____

_____

_____

2. Do you ever consider that God controls every detail, down to the number of seconds we sleep?

A. What is Samuel doing when God calls him (1 Sam. 3:1–10)?

> **3:1** Now the boy Samuel continued serving the Lord under Eli's supervision. Word from the Lord was rare in those days; revelatory visions were infrequent.
>
> **3:2** Eli's eyes had begun to fail, so that he was unable to see well. At that time he was lying down in his place, **3:3** and the lamp of God had not yet been extinguished. Samuel was lying down in the temple of the Lord as well; the ark of God was also there. **3:4** The

Lord called to Samuel, and he replied, "Here I am!" **3:5** Then he ran to Eli and said, "Here I am, for you called me." But Eli said, "I didn't call you. Go back and lie down." So he went back and lay down. **3:6** The Lord again called, "Samuel!" So Samuel got up and went to Eli and said, "Here I am, for you called me." But Eli said, "I didn't call you, my son. Go back and lie down."

3:7 Now Samuel did not yet know the Lord; the word of the Lord had not yet been revealed to him. **3:8** Then the Lord called Samuel a third time. So he got up and went to Eli and said, "Here I am, for you called me!" Eli then realized that it was the Lord who was calling the boy. **3:9** So Eli said to Samuel, "Go back and lie down. When he calls you, say, "Speak, Lord, for your servant is listening." So Samuel went back and lay down in his place.

3:10 Then the Lord came and stood nearby, calling as he had previously done, "Samuel! Samuel!" Samuel replied, "Speak, for your servant is listening!"

B. When does God give the psalmist a song (Ps. 42:8)?

Psalm 42:8 By day the Lord decrees his loyal love, and by night he gives me a song, a prayer to the living God.

C. Centuries before Esther, another Bible character experienced a reversal of circumstances when God spoke to a king in the night hours. Many see parallels between the two stories (those of Esther and Joseph). Read Genesis 41 and consider what happened?

Genesis 41:1 At the end of two full years Pharaoh had a dream. As he was standing by the Nile, **41:2** seven fine-looking, fat cows were coming up out of the Nile, and they grazed in the reeds. **41:3** Then seven bad-looking, thin cows were coming up after them from the Nile, and they stood beside the other cows at the edge of the river. **41:4** The bad-looking, thin cows ate the seven fine-looking, fat cows. Then Pharaoh woke up.

41:5 Then he fell asleep again and had a second dream: There were seven heads of grain growing on one stalk, healthy and good.

41:6 Then seven heads of grain, thin and burned by the east wind, were sprouting up after them. **41:7** The thin heads swallowed up the seven healthy and full heads. Then Pharaoh woke up and realized it was a dream.

41:8 In the morning he was troubled, so he called for all the diviner-priests of Egypt and all its wise men. Pharaoh told them his dreams, but no one could interpret them for him. **41:9** Then the chief cupbearer said to Pharaoh, "Today I recall my failures. **41:10** Pharaoh was enraged with his servants, and he put me in prison in the house of the captain of the guards—me and the chief baker. **41:11** We each had a dream one night; each of us had a dream with its own meaning. **41:12** Now a young man, a Hebrew, a servant of the captain of the guards, was with us there. We told him our dreams, and he interpreted the meaning of each of our respective dreams for us. **41:13** It happened just as he had said to us—Pharaoh restored me to my office, but he impaled the baker."

41:14 Then Pharaoh summoned Joseph. So they brought him quickly out of the dungeon; he shaved himself, changed his clothes, and came before Pharaoh. **41:15** Pharaoh said to Joseph, "I had a dream, and there is no one who can interpret it. But I have heard about you, that you can interpret dreams." **41:16** Joseph replied to Pharaoh, "It is not within my power, but God will speak concerning the welfare of Pharaoh."

D. Like Esther, Daniel lived in captivity outside of Israel during the time of exile. Read Daniel 2:1–20.

Daniel 2:1 In the second year of his reign Nebuchadnezzar had many dreams. His mind was disturbed and he suffered from insomnia. **2:2** The king issued an order to summon the magicians, astrologers, sorcerers, and wise men in order to explain his dreams to him. So they came and awaited the king's instructions.

2:3 The king told them, "I have had a dream, and I am anxious to understand the dream." **2:4** The wise men replied to the king: [What follows is in Aramaic] "O king, live forever! Tell your servants the dream, and we will disclose its interpretation." **2:5** The king replied to the wise men, "My decision is firm. If you do not inform me of both the dream and its interpretation, you will be dismembered and your homes reduced to rubble! **2:6** But if you can disclose the dream and its interpretation, you will receive from me gifts, a reward, and considerable honor. So disclose to me the dream and its interpretation!" **2:7** They again replied, "Let the king inform us of the dream; then we will disclose its interpretation." **2:8** The king replied, "I know for sure that you are attempting to gain time, because you see that my decision is firm. **2:9** If you don't inform me of the dream, there is only one thing that is going to happen to you. For you have agreed among yourselves to report to me something false and deceitful until such time as things might change. So tell me the dream, and I will have confidence that you can disclose its interpretation."

2:10 The wise men replied to the king, "There is no man on earth who is able to disclose the king's secret, for no king, regardless of his position and power, has ever requested such a thing from any magician, astrologer, or wise man. **2:11** What the king is asking is too difficult, and no one exists who can disclose it to the king, except for the gods—but they don't live among mortals!"

2:12 Because of this the king got furiously angry and gave orders to destroy all the wise men of Babylon. **2:13** So a decree went out, and the wise men were about to be executed. Then Daniel and his friends were sought so that they could be executed.

2:14 Then Daniel spoke with prudent counsel to Arioch, who was in charge of the king's executioners and who had gone out to execute the wise men of Babylon. **2:15** He inquired of the king's deputy, "Why is the decree from the king so urgent?" Then Arioch informed Daniel about the matter. **2:16** So Daniel went in and requested the king to grant him time, that he might disclose the interpretation to the king. **2:17** Then Daniel went to his home and informed his friends Hananiah, Mishael, and Azariah of the matter. **2:18** He asked them to pray for mercy from the God of heaven concerning this mystery so that he and his friends would not be destroyed with the rest of the wise men of Babylon. **2:19** Then in a night vision the mystery was revealed to Daniel. So Daniel praised the God of heaven, **2:20** saying, "Let the name of God be praised forever and ever, for wisdom and power belong to him.

E. How does the story above compare with those of Pharaoh and of King Xerxes? What do they all have in common? What do these stories teach us about God's control of events?

_____

_____

_____

THURSDAY: DIVINE IRONY

1. What is ironic about King Xerxes' and Haman's actions (Esther 5:14 and 6:1–6)?

_____

_____

_____

_____

2. Reread the ten verses that make up Esther 7. List circumstances that change drastically in this chapter.

_____

_____

A. What is the status of the woman who, along with her people, had been "sold to die" (7:2)?

_____

_____

B. What happens to the one who plotted against Esther's people (v. 10)?

_____

_____

C. What happens to the man who was so cocky the previous day (v. 6)?

_____

_____

_____

D. Where is Haman hanged (v. 9)?

_____

_____

_____

E. Herodotus records a time during the reign of Darius when a traitor's property was confiscated (*The Histories*, 3:128–9). What happens to Haman's property (8:7)?

_____

_____

_____

F. Esther starts out begging for her people to be spared. Who ends up begging at the end (v. 7)?

_____

_____

3. How do you see justice carried out in the lives of Esther, Mordecai, and Haman?

> When Haman realizes the trouble he's in, he begs the queen for mercy. In doing so he breaks a strict rule of court etiquette. To approach the queen or even speak to her is highly offensive. But to do so while the king is out of the room is unthinkable. Consider that the men who interact with the court women are eunuchs.

_____

_____

_____

4. Through the events in this section we continue to see God's sovereignty. Reflect on circumstances in your own life in which you'd like to see God perform some great reversals. Pray about these circumstances, thanking God for His sovereign care. If you are suffering an

injustice, commit yourself to letting Him exact justice rather than taking revenge.

_____

_____

_____

FRIDAY: THE PATIENCE OF GOD

1. The events in the story take place over a relatively long period of time. God is seemingly in no hurry, but slowly weaves events to bring about the best end. Note the markers in the book that indicate the passage of time.

A. In what year of King Ahasuerus' reign does the banquet take place (1:3)?

_____

_____

B. Note the month and year in which the king chooses Esther (2:16). How many years have passed since the deposing of Vashti and the king's choice of Esther?

_____

_____

_____

C. In what month and year of King Ahasuerus' reign is Haman's plot approved (3:7)?

_____

_____

D. How many months go by from the time of the plot's approval to the day when the Jews are to be killed (9:1)?

_____

E. Approximately how many years pass from the beginning of the book until the end of the main story?

_____

2. God provides for the Jews through the edict Mordecai issues in the king's name. How does the edict (8:11–13) provide what Esther wants (vv. 5–6) without reversing the first edict (3:9, 12–14)?

_____

_____

_____

3. Read 8:17 carefully. Becoming Jewish cannot mean changing one's lineage. It means converting to Judaism. Note how God has drawn people to himself even without using anyone who has been overtly walking in His ways. What does that say about Him?

_____

_____

_____

4. The author emphasizes three times that the Jews did not lay their hands on their enemies' plunder (9:10, 15, 16). Why might Esther's people have refrained from grasping their enemies' possessions, despite the king's permission to do so (8:11)?

_____

_____

_____

5. Mordecai and Esther establish the celebration of Purim as a holiday for their people. What is the purpose of the celebration (9:20–27) and how is it to be celebrated (9:22)?

_____

_____

6. Summarize what happens to Esther and Mordecai at the end of the story (9:29—10:3).

_____

_____

7. The Book of Esther has shown us God's providence and His faithfulness in the face of His people's unfaithfulness. Spend a few minutes thanking God for being in control, asking Him to enable you to stand faithfully. Praise Him for His ongoing faithfulness to you.

> Earlier we witnessed Saul's descent from a position of God's favor because he plundered the Amalekites rather than destroying their goods, as he was supposed to do (1 Sam. 15). Apparently Abraham's descendants remembered that incident and refused to take any spoil when participating in God's ultimate judgment on the Amalekites hundreds of years later. They restrained themselves, even when they had King Xerxes' permission to take what they wanted.

_____

_____

SATURDAY: ESTHER THE QUEEN

About ten years ago my husband, Gary, and a friend (both of German descent) had an overnight layover in Frankfurt, Germany. Wishing to make the most of their time, they decided to go out and see the city. So they asked the concierge about the best subway route to take, but the response they received stopped them in their tracks.

"I advise you not to go," the concierge said.

"Why not?"

"Because the skinheads are out tonight."

They gulped. "What?"

"Oh, excuse me!" he corrected himself. "You both look Aryan. You will have no problem."

Small comfort.

Prejudice, especially anti-Semitism, still thrives well over two thousand years after the first Feast of Purim. Consider six million Jews murdered in the last century. And let's not forget Saddam Hussein, whose rule was not exactly characterized by his love for Israelis.

It wasn't paranoia that drove Mordecai to advise Esther to conceal her identity. His concerns proved valid. Even though Esther was queen—quite a lofty position—she *still* wanted to keep her lineage under wraps. She hid her true identity because threats to her people were real. Yet when pushed into a corner, she chose to go public. Something subtle in the text signals a transformation in our reluctant hero once she makes up her mind to do so.

In the beginning she is called "Queen Esther" only once (2:22), and she is referred to as "the queen" once when she expresses her initial concern for Mordecai (4:4). But these are the only indications the text gives us about her royal position. Then something radically changes. After she fasts, makes up her mind to risk her life, and prepares a banquet for the king, she does something significant: she dons her royal robes (5:1).

What happens next?

The king, we are told, sees "Esther, the queen," and extends to her his scepter. "What is troubling you, *Queen Esther*?" he asks (italics mine). Then thirteen times throughout the remainder of the book, Esther is referred to as "the queen" or "Queen Esther."

In covering herself with the robes of her position and going to intercede for her people, Esther performs a symbolic act. She is not simply Esther, Queen of the Persians. She is Esther, queen of Abraham's descendants, identifying with her people to the point of death.

Where King Saul had failed to wipe out the Amalekites, Queen Esther was merciless. And the way the story is written, we are to interpret her ruthlessness toward Haman and his sons as good. King Saul started well yet ended badly. Queen Esther started on a questionable note yet ended quite well.

Ending well for Esther began when she decided to identify with her people, living in accordance with who she really was.

With whom do you identify? Through trusting Christ's atoning sacrifice on the cross, we identify with Christ's death and life. We do the same through the waters of baptism. And through partaking of the Lord's Supper, we identify with Christ's broken body, and His blood. We do so in community, identifying with the people of Christ—His church, the Body and Bride.

Sometimes it takes courage to identify ourselves with Christ. On the first day of a novel-writing class at a state university my professor announced, "I don't care if you write gay, lesbian, or porn; just don't give me anything Christian."

To some, Christians are odious because we've been arrogant. We've shown up making demands when we should have first asked questions. Yet many oppose Christ-followers out of sheer bias. Jesus told His disciples to expect this: "I have told you these things so that in me you may have peace. In the world you have trouble and suffering, but take courage—I have conquered the world" (John 16:33). Despite the challenges, we have royal pedigrees. We have more than enough resources to have courage, to take a stand, to end well. If we have trusted in Jesus' finished work on the cross, we have the right to be called children of God (John 1:12; Gal. 3:7). Sons. Daughters. Princes. Princesses.

Do you realize who you are?

Now go into the world in peace,
Have courage,
Hold on to what is good,
Honor all men,
Strengthen the faint-hearted,
Support the weak,
Help the suffering and share the Gospel.
Love and serve the Lord
In the power of the Holy Spirit and
May the grace of our Lord
Jesus Christ be with you all.
Amen.[7]

Prayer: *Almighty King and Father, thank You that I can trust Your sovereign plan even when circumstances seem to make no sense. Thank You for sending Your Son that I might have the opportunity to be Your child. Give me courage. Help me not to hide my spiritual heritage, but rather to*

[7] Traditional Anglican benediction.

identify with You and Your people shamelessly. Thank You for the story of Esther—for the reminder of how You keep Your promise to preserve Your people against all odds. Thank You that Your invisible hand directs every circumstance. Help me to trust and rest in Your unfailing love. These things I pray in Jesus' name, Amen.

For Memorization: "Compete well for the faith and lay hold of that eternal life you were called for and made your good confession for in the presence of many witnesses. I charge you before God who gives life to all things and Christ Jesus who made his good confession before Pontius Pilate, to obey this command without fault or failure until the appearing of our Lord Jesus Christ—whose appearing the blessed and only Sovereign, the King of kings and Lord of lords, will reveal at the right time. He alone possesses immortality and lives in unapproachable light, whom no human has ever seen or is able to see. To him be honor and eternal power! Amen." (1 Tim. 6:12–16)

About the NET BIBLE®

The NET BIBLE® is an exciting new translation of the Bible with 60,932 translators' notes! These translators' notes make the original Greek, Hebrew and Aramaic texts of the Bible far more accessible and unlocks the riches of the Bible's truth from entirely new perspectives.

The NET BIBLE® is the first modern Bible to be completely free for anyone, anywhere in the world to download as part of a powerful new "Ministry First" approach being pioneered at bible.org.

**Download the entire NET Bible and
60,932 notes for free at www.bible.org**

bible.org
Trustworthy Bible Study Resources™

About the bible.org ministry

Before there was eBay® . . . before there was Amazon.com® . . . there was bible.org! Bible.org is a non-profit (501c3) Christian ministry headquartered in Dallas, Texas. In the last decade bible.org has grown to serve millions of individuals around the world and provides thousands of trustworthy resources for Bible study (2 Tim 2:2).

**Go to www.bible.org for thousands
of trustworthy resources including:**

- The NET BIBLE®
- Discipleship Materials
- The Theology Program
- More than 10,000 Sermon Illustrations
- ABC's of Christian Growth
- Bible Dictionaries and Commentaries